I0417172

Editor-in-Chief and Founder:
  Lyndon H. LaRouche, Jr.
Editorial Board: *Lyndon H. LaRouche, Jr. , Helga
  Zepp-LaRouche, Paul Gallagher, Tony Papert,
  Gerald Rose, Dennis Small, Jeffrey Steinberg,
  William Wertz*
Co-Editors: *Paul Gallagher, Tony Papert*
Managing Editor: *Nancy Spannaus*
Technology: *Marsha Freeman*
Books: *Katherine Notley*
Ebooks: *Richard Burden*
Graphics: *Alan Yue*
Photos: *Stuart Lewis*
Circulation Manager: *Stanley Ezrol*

INTELLIGENCE DIRECTORS
Counterintelligence: *Jeffrey Steinberg, Michele
  Steinberg*
Economics: *John Hoefle, Marcia Merry Baker,
  Paul Gallagher*
History: *Anton Chaitkin*
Ibero-America: *Dennis Small*
Russia and Eastern Europe: *Rachel Douglas*
United States: *Debra Freeman*

INTERNATIONAL BUREAUS
Bogotá: *Miriam Redondo*
Berlin: *Rainer Apel*
Copenhagen: *Tom Gillesberg*
Houston: *Harley Schlanger*
Lima: *Sara Madueño*
Melbourne: *Robert Barwick*
Mexico City: *Gerardo Castilleja Chávez*
New Delhi: *Ramtanu Maitra*
Paris: *Christine Bierre*
Stockholm: *Ulf Sandmark*
United Nations, N.Y.C.: *Leni Rubinstein*
Washington, D.C.: *William Jones*
Wiesbaden: *Göran Haglund*

ON THE WEB
e-mail: eirns@larouchepub.com
www.larouchepub.com
www.executiveintelligencereview.com
www.larouchepub.com/eiw
Webmaster: *John Sigerson*
Assistant Webmaster: *George Hollis*
Editor, Arabic-language edition: *Hussein Askary*

EIR (ISSN 0273-6314) *is published weekly
(50 issues), by EIR News Service, Inc.,
P.O. Box 17390, Washington, D.C. 20041-0390.
(703) 777-9451*

European Headquarters: E.I.R. GmbH, Postfach
Bahnstrasse 9a, D-65205, Wiesbaden, Germany
Tel: 49-611-73650
Homepage: http://www.eirna.com
e-mail: eirna@eirna.com
Director: Georg Neudecker

Montreal, Canada: 514-461-1557

Denmark: EIR - Danmark, Sankt Knuds Vej 11,
basement left, DK-1903 Frederiksberg, Denmark.
Tel.: +45 35 43 60 40, Fax: +45 35 43 87 57. e-mail:
eirdk@hotmail.com.

Mexico City: EIR, Sor Juana Inés de la Cruz 242-2
Col. Agricultura C.P. 11360
Delegación M. Hidalgo, México D.F.
Tel. (5525) 5318-2301
eirmexico@gmail.com

Canada Post Publication Sales Agreement
#40683579

Postmaster: Send all address changes to *EIR*, P.O.
Box 17390, Washington, D.C. 20041-0390.

Signed articles in *EIR* represent the views of the
authors, and not necessarily those of the Editorial
Board.

Bringing the Rain

About This Issue

by Tony Papert

May 17—The report which follows below, by Ben Deniston, proves that even with the scientific knowledge already available (to some) today, we can bring water-vapor inland from over the oceans, and cause rainfall more or less when and where we want it,—never mind that the prospect provokes hysteria among many of our so-called scientists.

A second report shows that actual music has nothing in common with what most of today's audiences, and even professional musicians, think music is.

Putting these things together, I was forcefully reminded of an anecdote which *EIR* Editor-in-Chief Lyndon LaRouche had related in a 1998 paper published in *EIR*, Sept. 18, 1998 ("The

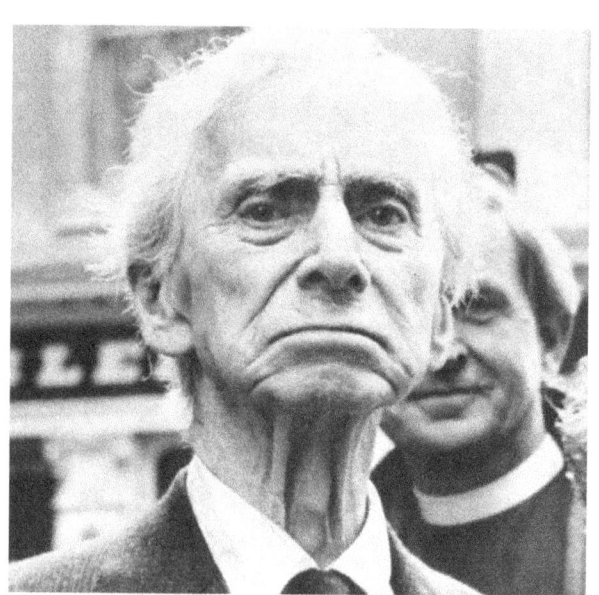 

Two diametrically opposed approaches: Bertrand Russell (left) vs. Alexander Hamilton (right).

Death-Agony of Olympus").Lyn's friend and co-worker for the Strategic Defense Initiative, the late French General G. Revault d'Allonnes, had told him of an incident from postwar Germany, when Revault d'Allonnes had been a "mere colonel," seated at the lowest-ranking position at a table of generals. In response to the question, "What is the first action we must take in the case of the outbreak of war," then-Colonel Revault d'Allonnes had created a sudden silence with his hubristic, "Fire all the generals!"

But in a discussion of this issue last Thursday (May 14), Lyn dismissed that metaphor. For the theme and introduction to the issue, he said, "The very idea is, they all want to come up from a mathematical approach as such, and they don't realize that the key thing is that you get a change in the modalities. A qualitative change in the modalities. They don't understand that. The basic essence of competent strategy, is always to go to a shift in the ontological characteristics of your action.

"They're idiots; they don't understand it. And most of our members are idiots.

"Make this the preface: this will simplify things. That's what the issue is about, under various topics and various guises; you just reaffirm it."

On the confused Congressmen who don't understand why Glass-Steagall is the one thing that they absolutely must do at this very moment, Lyn said:

The point is that the mathematics question comes up again, and that confuses everybody. If you look at Hamilton's writings: it's all there. But most of the people in the Congress are idiots; they have no notion of economy. It's their BRAINS which have been deduced.

What has been the problem? Isn't that the same thing as the Einstein issue? The Riemannian Revolution and Einstein's starting point at the end of the Nineteenth Century, were crushed by Hilbert and Russell in 1900. Hamilton's is a Riemannian system. There's probably just a tiny handful of scientific people, and some others, who can understand it.

How do you actually go from a sound physical economy, and go back into Hamilton? Hamilton in terms of modern economics is really original. If you read Hamilton's works, you can go way back into the history of science, back to Nicholas of Cusa and so forth.

In a discussion with another colleague the next day, Lyn dwelt at greater length on Hamilton's Principle as this sudden ontological upshifting. To begin solving the economic problem today, first you have to "strip out the fraud," he said, and Glass Steagall is the way to do it. Any other approach is garbage, and will not work.

Then, he said, you need a "surge of credit." But the credit is not just to fund "projects,—it is based on an anticipated development of the labor force,— we need a credit system to create a labor force." This is what is unique to Hamilton,—his understanding of credit as the means to develop the nation, through advances in real productivity. We cannot just use the BRICS "as a slogan,"—the issue with the BRICS "is the adoption of my (Lyn's) idea of credit, which is the Hamiltonian Principle—we cannot dilute this."

On California, you have to really hit this question of water. How can you have an aerospace sector in southern California, if there is no water,—have all the work done by robots? Then he discussed the importance of aerospace in the Northwest, where you still have some functioning plants. But we are losing the work force,—and yet the engineering and the technology is there, and could be used for many things. In Southern California, all you have are the "relics of aerospace."

This is how you use credit,—to advance those capabilities, by building up a qualified work force, as Franklin Roosevelt did. That's the only way to address the water crisis, as Ben Deniston has done,—by using the crisis to define the scientific work necessary to solve it. To get to this, you have to change the thinking, to understand the importance not just of a science driver, but of a labor force which can be deployed to develop it. This is what the thrust of our organizing must be.

"The solution is there,—we just have to tickle the galaxy to get it."

EIR Contents

www.larouchepub.com   Volume 42, Number 20, May 15, 2015

Cover
This Week

"Among the Sierra Nevada Mountains, California" by Albert Bierstadt, 1868

Bringing the Rain

The following was presented on the New Paradigm for Mankind weekly webcast on May 13, 2015, which featured Jason Ross, Megan Beets, and Ben Deniston of the LaRouche Scientific Basement Team.

Ben Deniston: I want to continue directly from last week on the theme of how to address the water crisis from this galactic perspective.

First, if people watching this haven't seen last week's show, they should definitely watch it—the May 6 edition. I'm going to continue from what was presented there. We're developing a completely new idea about how to manage water supplies. This is the type of science-driver program which a sane United States, under a sane leadership, in cooperation with other nations, would be taking up immediately.

Water is one of the major issues. Obviously we're hearing about California right now, facing a major crisis, a crisis that is accelerated by the fact that you have an insane governor there [Jerry Brown], whose response to the water crisis is to impose manadatory restrictions and move towards what is, in effect, a depopulation policy: a response to the water crisis by just saying, "Well, we have too many people, so let's just restrict use and let the weak ones weed themselves out under that policy." That's Brown's policy.

So, we have a major issue, accelerated by these types of insane, really genocidal leaders, like Brown and Obama.

But water is a major issue outside the United States, too. Many nations, many places around the world, are suffering a shortage of water, shortage of clean water, lack of water management. So, this is a central issue in the perspective we're talking about: the potential to get the United States to shift, and to break from the tradition of the past four terms of Presidents, and return to its roots as a republican nation, focused on science, into the development and cooperation with other nations in that regard.

In dealing with this water issue, what we've been defining is a new perspective for how to manage the water systems. We're looking at going beyond just managing water supplies that arc on the ground, shifting water around, things that, in those terms, are going to need to be done: We're going to need to manage rivers, and ground water supplies, and lakes, and so forth. But what we're looking at now is the potential to subsume that within an entirely new perspective: managing the water of the atmosphere; managing weather systems; managing the behavior of atmospheric water vapor on regional and potentially larger scales—to provide a completely new method of control over the water cycle, and developing the water system of the planet for the needs of mankind.

The Galactic Perspective

Last week we defined the galactic perspective on the water system.[1] We looked at all these correlations, these cycles and fluctuations, in climate records and in the behavior of water, and the behavior of the climate going back decades, hundreds of years, thousands of years, millions of years, tens of millions of years. And you see all these variations in temperature, glaciation, rainfall, all these aspects of climate and the water cycle. And we

---

1. May 6, 2015 New Paradigm for Mankind show (www.YouTube.com/Watch?v=dth3hPr-PEA), published in the May 15, 2015 issue of EIR, "Galactic Man: Shadow versus Principle."

Spiral galaxy NGC 6744, thought to be quite similar to the Milky Way which encompasses our Solar System

European Southern Observatory

see in all these scales, that these variations correspond with changes in the influence of cosmic factors: how the Sun is behaving, what the Sun is doing.

And also, most importantly for our perspective here, variations in the influence from the galaxy, from the galactic system. We see direct relations between these aspects of the behavior of the water cycle, and the amount of so-called galactic cosmic radiation intersecting the Earth, interacting with the Earth—variations in the effect of the galactic system.

What we defined last week is really the need to reconceptualize our understanding of this atmospheric system that we're living in: that it's not just an Earth-based system. It's not even just an Earth-Sun system, but it is, in part at least, significantly a galactic environment. That the characteristics of our atmosphere are being shaped constantly by the high-energy radiation, the effect, of the galactic system around us, constantly flooding the atmosphere, affecting the conditions, certain qualities of the atmosphere, which play an important role in affecting how water vapor behaves.

Last week we defined that from the standpoint of these longer-term correlations, and also very short-term effects, where you see, on the scale of days, rapid changes in the influence of the galaxy, as can be created by outbursts of Solar activity, which can kind of shield the Earth from galactic activity, and its galactic cosmic radiation. And then right after that, looking on the scale of days, you see atmospheric conditions, conditions of water vapor in the atmosphere, changing, in direct response to this shift in the amount of galactic influence, so to speak.

So you're starting to develop this picture: that we're living in this system which is, in part, created and molded and shaped by this high-energy influence from the galaxy. So that we're living in a galactic atmosphere, a galactic environment. That's the condition that we exist in. And if we want to better understand water, and the water cycle—how water behaves—and climate and weather and related things, we have to now think about it from that standpoint. And I think, last week, we did a decent job in going through the evidence to paint that picture.

Atmospheric Ionization

What I want to take up today is, how can we then use that insight, to manage these conditions, to allow us to better control the water cycle from that standpoint.

What we're going to discuss is a number of examples of utilizing so-called atmospheric ionization systems to stimulate our own version of these types of effects on the atmosphere. That, as we discussed last week, one of the critical factors in the galactic influence, is that it is constantly creating a certain amount of ionization in the lower atmosphere, which plays a critical role in helping water vapor condense from a gas state to a liquid state, and form clouds, create precipitation, and related phenomena.

With that understanding, there have already been *decades* of experiments and demonstrations showing that we can create our own variations of these effects; we can create our own ionization effects on the atmosphere which, in a really interesting way, simulate, or you could say, allow us to manage, these galactic-type conditions in our atmosphere.

I want to show this one illustration (**Figure 1**) of one variation of these types, which we're going to discuss:

FIGURE 1

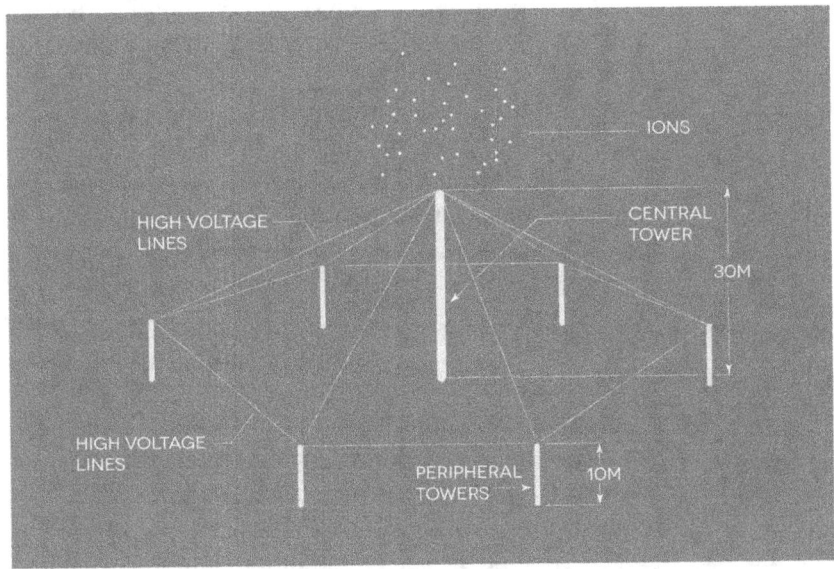

where they've been used, what the results have been, and what the potential is, so far, from what we know from these systems.

The basic idea is actually rather simple. This is a system of towers. You have a central tower, somewhere in the range of 30 meters (around 100 feet high), and then you have a series of smaller towers, around 10 meters high, surrounding it. These towers are then connected with rather thin wires, and through these wires, if you run the right high-voltage current, you can create an increase in the ionization effect in the surrounding atmosphere: what's called a Corona discharge effect.

By running the right kind of electrical current, high enough voltage, you can increase the rate of ionization, the amount of ionization effect, in the surrounding atmosphere.

None of these stations is really that big; you're talking about 30 meters high, surrounded by a series of towers, but they've been able to directly measure the effects of this, tens of miles away. So you can create a sphere of influence on a decent scale with just one of these systems, with a relatively low power input. So, you're utilizing these systems to manage the ionization and electrical conditions, in kind of a bubble, or section of the atmosphere, influenced by these stations, which give us at least an initial ability to begin to manage and control these conditions: the conditions that we discussed last week are critical in effecting how water vapor behaves, when it decides to move towards precipitation, when it doesn't—these types of things.

In theory, if this ionization, whether from the galaxy or whether from man-made systems, plays such a critical role in affecting how water behaves in the atmosphere, we should be able to utilize this to increase precipitation, for example. And this is what has been done.

There is a history to this which actually goes beyond my knowledge. There's a lot of work on this. I'm going to go through what I'm familiar with—a few places where this has been developed, a few particular groupings which worked on this technology—but I should emphasize that studies on this go back, even further back, to the 1940s. It's been tried in various ways. It's been tried in various forms. There's a whole interesting history to managing these ionization systems.

But what I want to focus in on, is, initially, technology that was developed in the Soviet Union in the mid-1980s. And I've seen reference to the initial development of this particular line of the technology at the Laboratory of Meteorological Protection of the City of Moscow. It's a rather interesting name for a laboratory. And I guess this was associated with, or paired with, the City Hall of Moscow.

So, in the mid-'80s, they started to work on weather modification, weather control systems, utilizing these types of technologies, these ionization effects. And they developed their first active system, I think, somewhere around 1986, technology that came to be referred to as ELAT, which stands for the Electrification of the Atmosphere.

I haven't actually been to see a whole lot of details on the operations in Moscow, but it was cited to have had some beneficial effects, managing the weather conditions for the city.

When the Soviet Union fell, in the early '90s, some of the people involved in this, began promoting this technology for use in other places, and you had, in particular, by the mid-'90s, some support for this developing in Mexico. You had the mayor of Mexico City at the time supporting it. You had some support from the head of the Mexican Senate Committee on Science and Technology, and then also some university scientists interested in it, supporting it, and then also some business support. So these different groupings came together, and funded and supported an initial trial program, to build some of these

FIGURE 2

ionization systems in Mexico, and see if they could get them to work—to be successful in increasing rainfall, especially in the desert regions of Mexico.

The initial trials were successful enough that they went from something like three stations, in the very late '90s, like 1999, up to 21 stations in 2004. So they were able to show enough success with their initial trials to get pretty decent expansion in the number of these stations. Here's an image of one of the stations operating in Mexico (**Figure 2**). You can see the central tower there. It might be difficult to see the wires coming off of the tower, because they're rather thin, so they're a little bit hard to pick up there.

And you see the small station where you operate the conditions of the system.

And then here's a display (**Figure 3**) of not all of the stations they have, but one set of some of the different locations where they had these systems built and operating.

And one thing they were trying to do with these systems—I think it's a critical part of the potential of this technology—is that they were able to utilize an array of these stations, starting near the coast, and moving further inland, to create the conditions to try to pull water vapor inland, from over the oceans. So, actually working to create a net flow of new atmospheric moisture over the land, which normally wouldn't be there under natural conditions.

And the way they were working with this was to try to utilize the effects of this ionization, the effects of the condensation of water vapor, to create small variations in the pressure, the atmospheric pressure. And by doing this, they could then create conditions where some of this water vapor would flow toward lower-pressure regions, further inland, so creating, in effect, an atmospheric canal, maybe you could say, bringing in a whole stream of new atmospheric water, atmospheric moisture, inland.

This is critical. Because otherwise, if you're just talking about getting existing water vapor to fall as rain, or precipitation—that can be useful; but you're not necessarily increasing the net amount of water coming into the continent, coming into the water cycle, over land. If you're operating with this kind of approach, you're attempting to actually draw in new sources of atmospheric moisture, and I think that's a critical aspect of how we want to work to develop these systems, because you're increasing the net amount of freshwater input into the continental system.

FIGURE 3

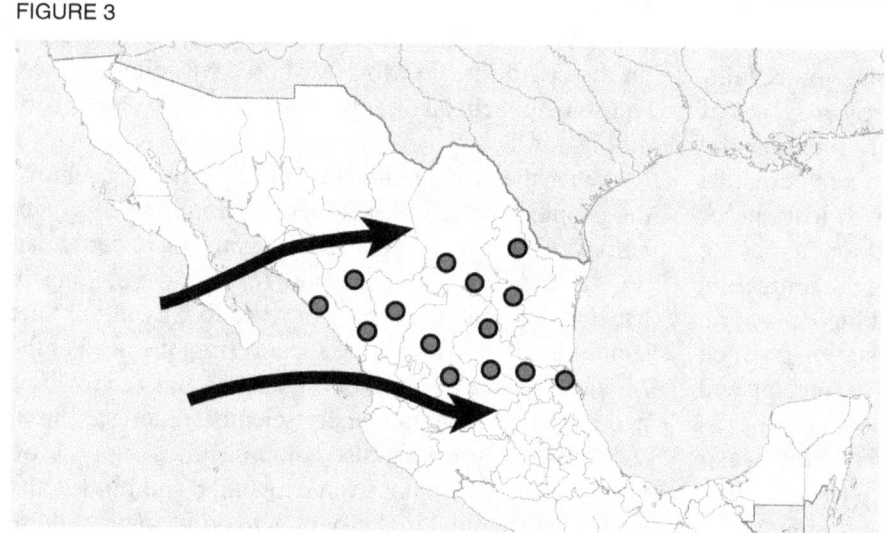

We've cited some of these figures before, but 90% of the water that's evaporated from the ocean, never makes it over land. It just falls back over the ocean again, so there's a huge potential in the water vapor system, naturally occurring, that these types of things begin to tap into, and draw a little bit more of that inland. Draw it inland, get it to fall over land, fill reservoirs, fill groundwater stores, fill lakes, rivers, participate in life and human activity, and then flow back into the ocean again, so we can increase the net flow of the cycle.

Anyway, that's the kind of concept they were working with in Mexico.

The Results in Mexico

Now I want to go through a quick series of some of the results, to show what they've been able to do with these systems. Here is a graphic of operations from 1999 to 2003 in the state of Durango, a state in Mexico (**Figure 4**). You can see the state highlighted in gray down there at the bottom. You can see it's situated with a few of these stations in the state, plus a station closer to the coast, to kind of create this draft effect, this pressure gradient to bring water further inland.

What we see in the chart on the top there, is a range of predictions for what they expected the rainfall to be, the precipitation to be, each year. So you have in the purple, the lower estimate; the green, the higher estimate. So you get a range for what they thought would be the lowest or highest amount of precipitation they could expect each year.

Jason Ross: Not using the system.

Deniston: Not using the system, yes. It's what they would expect the natural precipitation to be.

So, that's what they expected. But then, when utilizing the system, the actual rainfall in the states was measured in blue. So you can see: '99, 2000, 2001, 2002, 2003—in five consecutive years of utilizing the systems, you had consistently significant increase in the precipitation above what was expected for the state of Durango.[2]

I don't have a graphic for it, but there is reporting of their activity in the state of Sonora, where on average, they expected about 10 inches of rainfall each year; under the first year of operation of these systems, they had 51 inches of rainfall. So, a fivefold increase in rainfall above what the regular average is.

The following year they didn't utilize the systems. The rainfall that year was 11 inches. The next year they turned the station back on, and they had 47 inches of

FIGURE 4

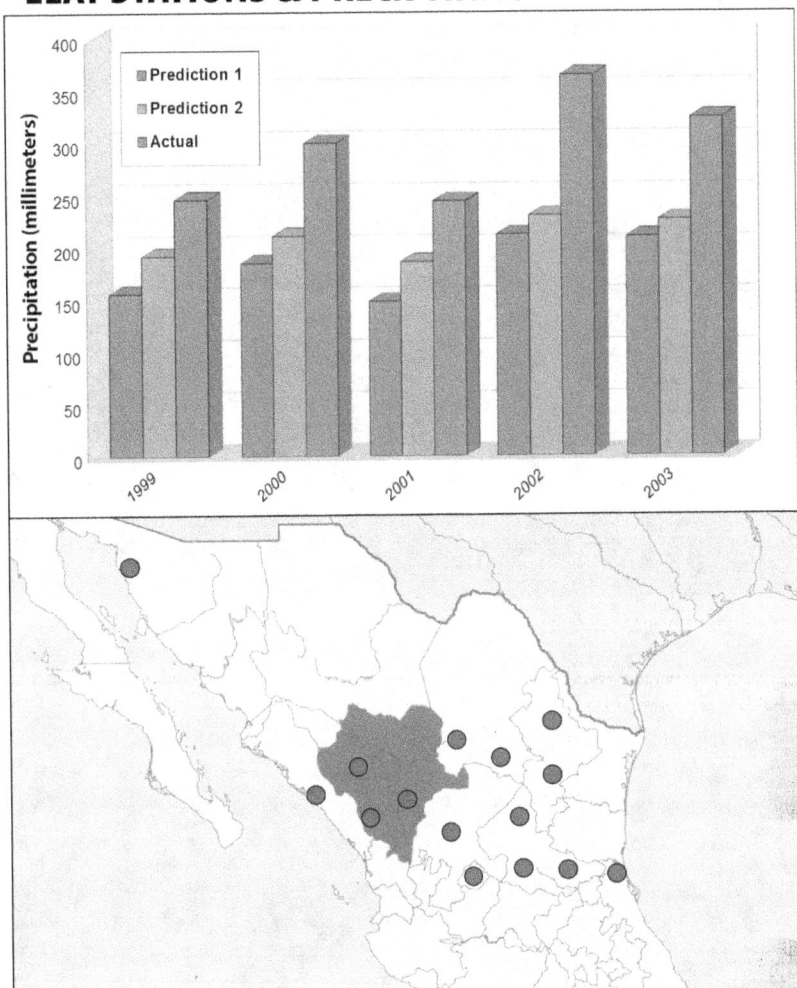

ELAT STATIONS & PRECIPITATION IN DURANGO

rainfall. So that was in Sonora, toward the north Pacific coast there.[3]

Other coverage in the *IEEE Spectrum* cited the effects on agriculture, and they said, in agricultural regions, you had a 61% increase in grain production, in regions that were affected by these systems. Obviously, increased precipitation helps agriculture, better agricultural growth, etc. So, these are some of the results cited.[4]

Here's another graphic (**Figure 5**).

Ross: I'm glad the bean-counters are put to productive work.

2. "Artificial Atmospheric Ionization: A Potential Window for Weather Modification," by Phillip Kauffman and Arquimedes Ruiz-Columbié, 16th Conference on Planned and Inadvertent Weather Modification.

3. "Looking for a Change in the Weather?" Jay Rizoli, Mass High Tech: *The Journal of New England Technology*, March 10th, 2003.

4. "Electrical Rainmaking Technology Gets Mexico's Blessing: But for Now, Doubters Prevail North of the Boarder," Samuel K Moore, *IEEE Spectrum*, April 2004.

FIGURE 5

Increase in Precipitation in States with Ionization Systems

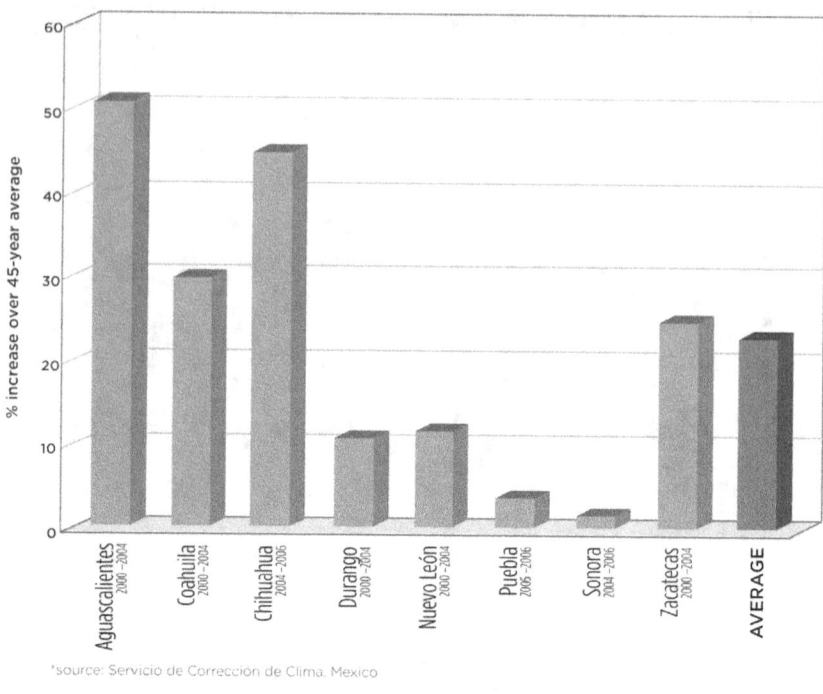

'source: Servicio de Correccion de Clima. Mexico

FIGURE 6

Deniston: Right. They were getting off easy. Got to give them something to do.

Here's a whole number of states, comparing the increased precipitation in each of these states, during the time that these stations were operational, when the atmospheric ionization, the weather-control stations, were operational, comparing the percentage of precipitation increase over the 45-year average of rainfall for those states.[5]

So, for example, on the far left, in this particular state, they had a certain amount of rainfall expected, based on the 45-year average. You just take the last 45 years, how much rain fell in the state, average it out for that whole time, and you get a nice long average for the amount of precipitation you would expect. But then from 2000 to 2004, in this particular case, they used the ELAT stations, and for that four-year period, on average, they got a 50% increase; they had rainfall for those four years, 50% higher than the entire 45-year average before that.

And that's recorded—each of these bars is for an individual state, under the influence of these systems. So, we looked at Durango: Here we see Durango—the fourth from the left—showing on average a 10% increase, from 2000 to 2004, under the influence of these systems, compared to what the average rainfall had been 45 years prior.

Ross: That's a smaller increase than the previous graph showed, right?

Deniston: It's pretty close. You mean this graph (Figure 4)?

Ross: Yes. That was just comparing estimates for those years, as opposed to 45 years earlier. That's why there's a difference.

Deniston: Yes, right. They estimated—however they did it—each of the years individually.

So, that's the precipitation increase. We were talking about Sonora, Durango; here's an array of other states showing average increases in precipitation (Figure 5).

They were also able to utilize this specifically, not just to increase overall precipitation generally, but to target particular reservoirs, particular basins, and watershed areas, where rainfall, precipitation, will feed into known rivers, which will feed into known reservoirs, and actually fill targeted reservoirs.

5. Fundación para Revertir el Calentamiento Global A.C., http://revirtiendoelcalentamientoglobal.org/index.php/correccion-clima

FIGURE 7

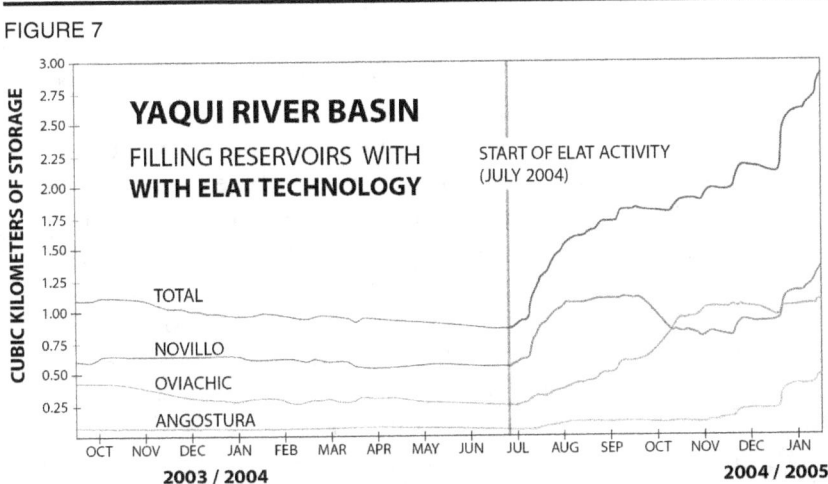

YAQUI RIVER BASIN

FILLING RESERVOIRS WITH **WITH ELAT TECHNOLOGY**

START OF ELAT ACTIVITY (JULY 2004)

TOTAL

NOVILLO

OVIACHIC

ANGOSTURA

2003 / 2004   2004 / 2005

FIGURE 8

Increase in Storage Utilization of Reservoirs Using Ionization Systems

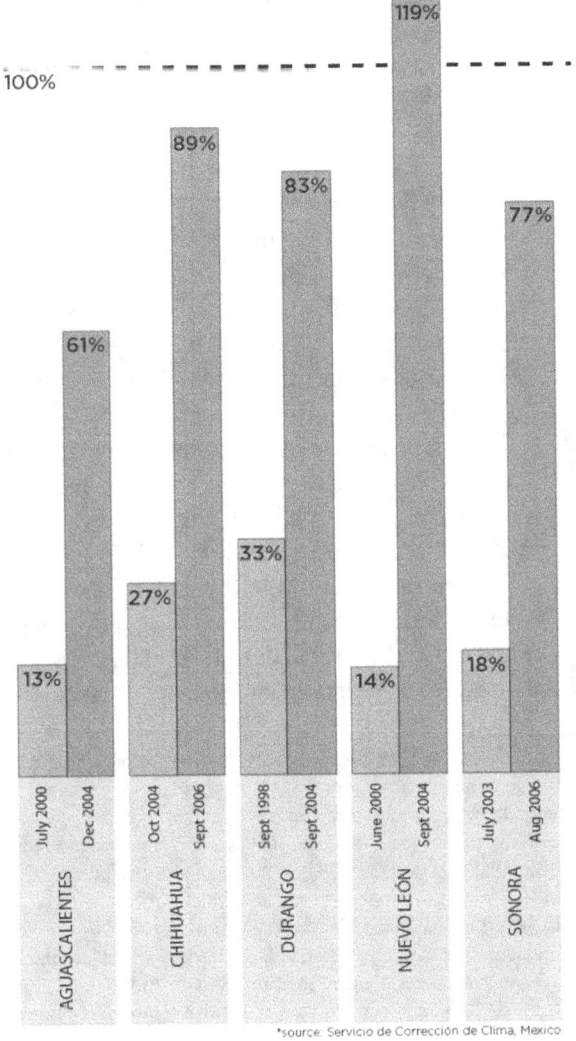

*source: Servicio de Corrección de Clima, Mexico

So, for example: This is a very simple general illustration of the river basin for the Yaqui River in northwestern Mexico (**Figure 6**). And utilizing these stations, they were able to significantly increase how filled these reservoirs were, under the operation of these ELAT systems. Here you have three reservoirs in that basin, indicated in the green, the gray, and the blue lines (**Figure 7**). And then the red line above that is the total amount for all those reservoirs added together.

And you can see: On the left here, going from toward the end of 2003, into the beginning of 2004, we have the reservoir levels as they were, without the influence of these weather control systems, these ELAT systems. And then, in July 2004, they began to utilize these systems in the region, with the particular goal of filling these reservoirs. And you can see rather clearly, timed with the beginning utilization of these systems, the level of the reservoirs began to rise in all three of them, and in the total.

So, you can see that, under the influence of these systems, the increased rainfall, you can utilize this increased rainfall to fill reservoir stores, to provide water for the existing water infrastructure systems.

This is one particular basin, a few reservoirs, in the state of Sonora.

Here's another graphic (**Figure 8**) illustrating the effect of filling reservoirs in a number of different states, around the nation of Mexico.[6] The red shows how full the reservoirs were before the utilization of these systems; the blue shows how full the reservoirs were after the utilization of these stations. So, on the right, to give an example, that's in the state of Sonora. So, the red there indicates the reservoir level in July 2003—it's about 18% full. Three years later, after a few years of utilizing these systems, the reservoir level went to 77% full, as measured in August 2006. You see a similar result for different states.

They've also been used to reduce forest fires. By increasing the precipitation in certain very dry regions, you can reduce the number of forest fires—those that get started, you can weaken them; you can prevent them from ever occurring. So here (**Figure 9**) we see indication of—again, under the effect of these stations, against

6. Information from Mexico's Agrifood and Fisheries Information Service and National Water commission.

FIGURE 9

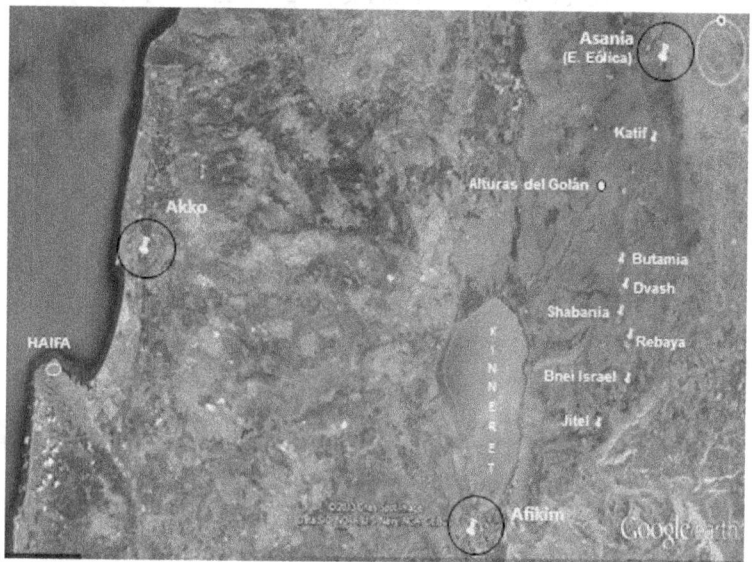

DISMINUCIÓN DE INCENDIOS CON IONIZACIÓN
[Reduction of Fires with Ionization]
1990 - 2006

	STATES
- 100 %	
- 3 %	AGUASCALIENTES
- 51 %	CHIHUAHUA
- 41 %	COAHUILA
- 47 %	DURANGO
- 97 %	NUEVO LEÓN
- 31 %	PUEBLA
- 3 %	SONORA
-70 %	ZACATECAS

CONAFOR

FIGURE 10

FIGURE 11

Welcome to Meteo Systems

some historical average of the number of forest fires in the area, the forest fires occurring in these states, you see it reduced, during the time period when they had these systems operational.[7] On average, you had traditionally a certain number of fires occurring in each of these regions, and they were able to utilize these systems down there, to get a reduction in the number of forest fires.

So, it's kind of an overview, over a decade of operations of these systems in Mexico.

Unfortunately, somewhat amazingly, despite this success, despite all this work that was done developing dozens of stations, consistent beneficial effects, they actually lost support in Mexico, and weren't able to continue operating there. There was opposition from certain elements of the government in other places to their work. We might mention that a little more throughout the discussion, but this stuff—people can probably imagine—is highly contested and debated by certain people who just axiomatically believe this could never happen. We can't influence the weather, etc., etc.

Beyond Mexico

So, unfortunately, they lost support for the activity in Mexico. This particular grouping then went over to Israel, found support in Israel, and from 2011 to 2013, fulfilled a contract to develop three stations (**Figure 10**). See the push pins, with the black circles around them. So, the top right, middle left, bottom center there—they built three stations, targeted to fill seven reservoirs in the Golan Heights region. The seven reservoirs are named there, along the righthand side.[8]

Then they were able to utilize these systems over a three-year period to successfully, significantly increase the volume of these reservoirs, and fill these reservoirs in Israel. And this particular

---

7. Information from the National Forestry Commission of Mexico, presented by Fundación para Revertir el Calentamiento Global A.C., http://revirtiendoelcalentamientoglobal.org/index.php/correccion-clima
8. Information from the Israel National Water Company and the Israel Meteorological Service, presented in "Inducción Experimental De Lluvias Por Ionización Atmosférica En Las Alturas Del Golán, Israel, En El Período Invernal 2012-2013," Mario Dominguez and Lev Pokhmelnykh, Science, Technology And Innovation For Development Of Mexico, (http://pcti.mx/) http://pcti.mx/articulos/item/induccion- experimental-de-lluvias-por-ionizacion- atmosferica-en-las-alturas-del-golan-israel-en-el-periodo-invernal-2012-2013

FIGURE 12

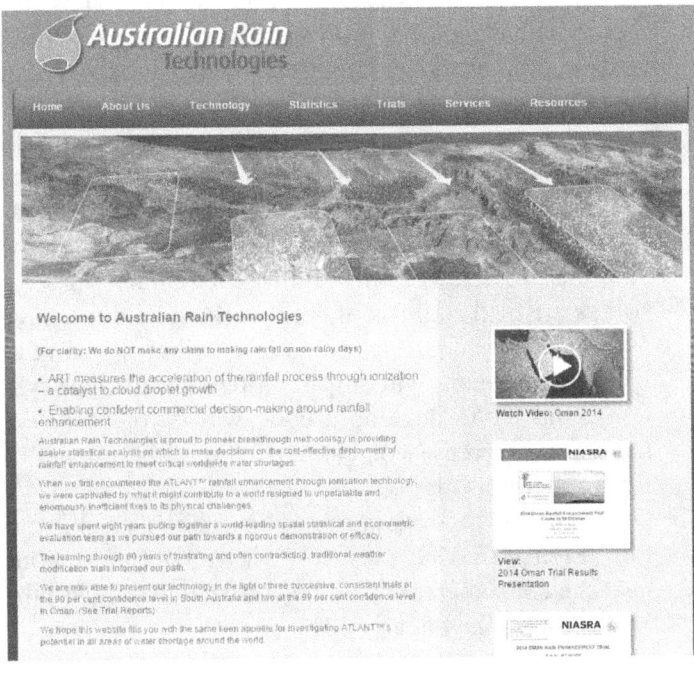

FIGURE 13

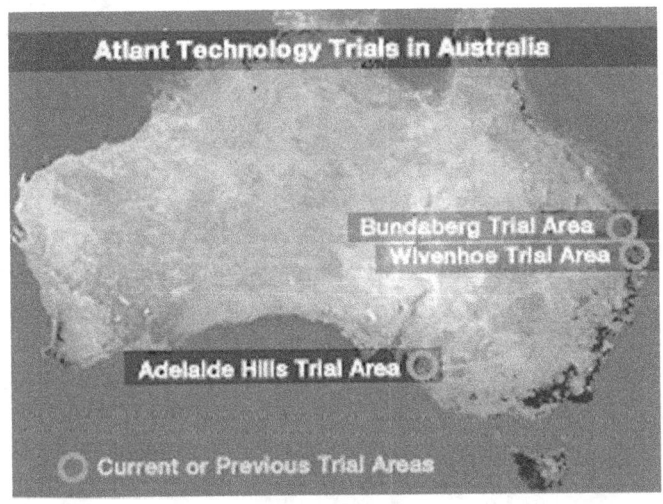

grouping is still working on the technology there in Israel, developing it, refining it. And they have interest from nations in Asia in developing the technology in Asia, and bringing it there. So they're working on pursuing the development of the technology there.

So, that's one whole historical arc. You had this Russian grouping, led by certain scientists in Russia. They were able to develop and utilize this technology in Mexico, and then we saw the results. They went to Israel; we saw successful results there. So, that's one outfit that exists that's utilized these systems to increase

rainfall, to have these beneficial effects.

Now I want to highlight another company, separate from the company I just discussed, called Meteo Systems (**Figure 11**). This company was formed in Switzerland. They did some initial trials, demonstrations of some basic technology, similar technology, in Switzerland in 2006. This was then brought to the Middle East, developed in the United Arab Emirates (UAE), utilized there to increase rainfall, provide certain beneficial effects there.[9] And then also, there was a spinoff company in Australia, which came out of Meteo Systems, a new company called Australian Rain Technologies.[10] And here's their website (**Figure 12**).

Instead of focusing on going right to commercial operations, and trying to sell this stuff, this company has been more focused on some very rigorous trials: to develop these systems, utilize them, show that we can increase the rainfall, show what the effects are, and demonstrate the technology for the many people who are still very hesitant to believe we can do this kind of stuff.

So, in Australia, starting in 2007, they ran a series of trials (**Figure 13**). First, in 2007 in Wivenhoe, which is on the far right, they did a trial, generating a 30% increase in precipitation in the region targetted by their area, compared to some of the surrounding areas. It was kind of a control. And it was also 12% higher precipitation than the historical average.

Based on the success in that, they had a second trial starting in 2008, at Bundaberg, which is north of the first trial area, where they were able to generate a 25% increase in precipitation in 2008. This also led to the development of another three years of trials in Southern Australia, the location indicated there, where in 2008, they generated a 15% increase in rainfall; 2009, a 10% increase; 2010, an 11% increase. So, a different company, different variation on the technology, but still showing some pretty consistent results. They can get a positive effect—about a 10% increase in rainfall.[11]

And as far as I've seen, they are actually utilizing systems that are operating on a little bit smaller scale than the activity in Mexico.

But, based on this success, in Australia over these

9. www.Meteo-Systems.com

10. http://www.australianrain.com.au/

11. Information and documentation on their Australian trials is available at http://australianrain.com.au/trials/

FIGURE 14

2014 OMAN RAIN ENHANCEMENT TRIAL

FINAL REPORT

February 2015

FIGURE 15

3.2.   Instrumentation of the trial

3.2.1.   ATLANT™ Sites

Two new ATLANT™ sites (H3 and H4) were chosen to supplement the two ATLANT™ sites (H1 and H2) used in 2013 (Figures 3-2 to 3-5). The sites were chosen based upon the following criteria:

· The sites were as similar as possible, in terms of meteorological conditions, and elevation

· The ATLANT™ systems were separated sufficiently from each other, such that their areas of influence did not significantly overlap

· The sites are located such that a line joining them runs at 90° to the major wind direction and so are located to take advantage of orographic lifting of the ion plume

· Surface-based measurements exist in the expanded trial area (e.g. rain gauge sites)

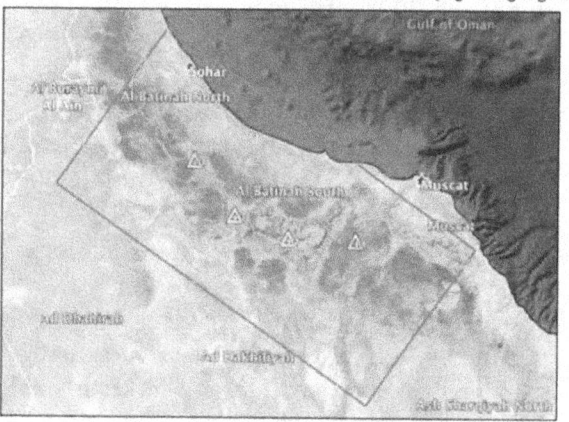

Figure 3-1 The ATLANT™ sites in the 2014 trial (shown as yellow triangles)

four years, they've gotten support for a new trial program in Oman, on the Arabian Peninsula, running from 2013 to 2018. So, they're two years into a new trial, a five-year trial program.

This is from their website (**Figure 14**); people can get their reports—Australian Rain Technologies. So they now have results from the first two years of their trials in Oman, and again, 2013, the first year, they got an 18% increase in rainfall. In the second year under operation, 2014, we got an 18 1/2% increase in rainfall. And part of this Oman trial is, they're working with independent scientists from some universities in Australia to do an independent assessment of their technology. And they're also very heavily focused on having very solid statistical analysis of their work, so you can have as good an estimate as possible of what the rainfall would have been, without the utilization of their systems, and try to develop a good way to measure the amount of increase you can attribute to the impact of their operations there.[12]

So, this is an ongoing program. Here's an illustration (**Figure 15**) of the last year's set-up of four stations near the coast there, which they utilized to increase the rainfall by nearly 20%.

The Oman trials are ongoing. They're still working on it in Israel. This is another company called Rain on Request (**Figure 16**)—good name—which is offering their technology to people in the United States.[13] They're campaigning, they're lobbying, to get state governments, counties, businesses, to get support to develop the technology in the United States. There are other companies that are currently pursuing the potential to develop this technology in Asia. Other companies are pursuing active interest in South America, in developing new implementations of these systems, related technologies.

So, this is not something that was done once somewhere, that had some vague results. This has been done in a number of nations, a number of different locations. It's still being developed, still being pursued, and there's active interest and support in expanding this in different places around the world.

This is a very exciting, interesting perspective. It's stuff we've been looking at now for a couple years, kind of following this with interest—that you're getting these consistent positive results from these ionization systems, to manage

12. "2014 Oman Rain Enhancement Trial Final Report," http://australianrain.com.au/assets/files/downloads/oman-2014-trial-report.pdf
13. www.RainOnRequest.com

FIGURE 16

RAIN (ON) REQUEST

RAIN ON REQUEST

- Most efficient weather control system on the planet requiring less equipment and power to induce more rainfall
- Does not use chemicals to enhance rainfall
- Provides targeted rainfall allowing for induced rainfall in specific regions
- Quick set up/breakdown
- Does not require clouds to induce rainfall unlike cloud seeding and other weather control systems

LATEST NEWS   NAVIGATION

the water cycle, increase the rainfall, utilize these things to tackle droughts, tackle wildfires, various aspects of weather and related conditions, by managing these atmospheric qualities of the water cycle.

A Science-Driver Program

I think the most important thing, going back to last week's show—you've been taken through a certain picture of some of the results that have been demonstrated, that show these systems have been able to consistently show positive results. I think the most important thing is to bring this back to this galactic perspective, on the program we're talking about here. You return to what we were talking about last week. We're living in the conditions of our galactic system, that is shaping these qualities of atmosphere. This is shaping and defining the conditions which affect and control how water behaves in the atmospheric system.

So, we're literally living in the field of influence of our galaxy. We're living in the galactic atmosphere right now, that's shaping the conditions we're experiencing and dealing with. But based on that insight, understanding that, and generating similar conditions, similar effects, affecting these conditions, affecting these ionization conditions our own way, under our own control, is showing us that we can have our own ability to manage these processes, manage these interactions, to control the water cycle, to control the weather, to generate precipitation, to manage conditions of the climate.

I think this defines an incredibly important perspec-

tive, because, putting together a crash program to pursue these weather-control systems, to really develop this technology to the fullest extent possible—I think what we're looking at here, is that you go to the case of California. We should be supporting a whole array of these systems. Any company that's shown decent results—and, as I went through, there are a few of them out there now—they should all be given support to develop their systems. And we should have rigorous trials to see whose systems work the best. Under what conditions do they work the best? Let them set up a number of systems, and run them under different conditions, under different power strength, voltage levels. To better experiment and understand: How can we to the fullest degree utilize these systems?

That has, at the same time, two critical benefits. One, obviously, the practical thing: We can provide water. We can save California. We can provide water for places that desperately need it. But two, this is a whole other experimental approach for understanding the nature of our galactic environment. Instead of just sitting back and speculating on a blackboard about how galactic cosmic rays might affect the atmosphere, from the standpoint of equations that you already believe in—why not actually take an experimental approach, and start to manage these conditions? That's going to give us all kinds of new insights into how to best understand the role of this influence in climate, in weather, how it affects our Earth system.

We're defining here a very clear science-driver program, where, in pursuing these things with a real crash program, hand in hand as we're expanding our ability to manage these systems for the benefit of mankind, at the same time, we're potentially expanding our understanding of the galactic system; the nature of the interaction between the galactic system with the Earth.

I think the most important thing that we're looking at here, is the galactic perspective: that we're looking at mankind redefining his understanding of the system we live in, as defined by the galactic processes, and in that way, being able to have completely new potentials for managing the systems on Earth.

There's a lot more that could be said, but, in direct continuation from last week, I think we're defining a very clear direction, of where we actually need to go.

What Is Music Really?

by Lyndon H. LaRouche, Jr.

The following is adapted from a discussion that Lyndon LaRouche had with associates following an informal evening of music on May 10, 2015.

Take the Schubert Ninth Symphony, conducted by [Wilhelm] Furtwängler.[1] You have everything in there which is required in that nature, and it occurred in a certain period of his life where he was totally dedicated to get this mission across. Why would he pick the Schubert symphony—why would he do that? His direction of the Schubert symphony was something absolutely unique, nobody ever did it properly again. And after the greatest musicians had heard it, they knew that Furtwängler was the only one who really owned that symphony.

So, the point is that, it's the mental condition: If you think that you, by some mathematical magic, have turned a score into music, you are—forgive my statement—full of shit. Because it doesn't work! Because the great compositions, if they are indeed great, don't do that. They don't try to do that.

Furtwängler's performance is a very clinically crucial thing. Everything about that is total suspension. And the suspension is totally controlled. When you hear, experience, the Furtwängler version, and you hear it in reasonable concern, you do not hear it in sections.

Wilhelm Furtwängler rehearses Beethoven's Symphony No. 2 with the Berlin Philharmonic Orchestra, February 1948.

You have a kind of religious experience, which starts out, in a sense, instructing you morally, at an opening. And then it goes through—like the second movement—it goes in a certain way which is almost magical. And most people, as conductors, couldn't do it. They butcher it, with rhythmic routines. They don't see where the progress is, in the process of that movement. They don't see the daring explosion, which is effected by Furtwängler's direction, at that point. And then the finale, the effect of that—Boom! Boom, Boom! This is charged! This is really Schubert.

I know of the mystery of this thing. I just worked at it for some time. It's a kind of thing which people call "religious." But what happens is, the people say, "well, this is religious." They may be Satanic, but this is not true religion.

---

1. The recording referenced here, "Schubert: Symphony No. 9 / Haydn: Symphony No. 88," Furtwängler/Berlin Philharmonic Orchestra, is available from Amazon.com.

Because if you want to actually compose something actually worth performing, and if you want to perform it in a way that does not butcher it, or butcher its intention, you have to give way to a meaning of your life. And the difference is, the average person thinks that they're born and they die, and they organize their lives on the basis of this idea, "I'm going to live until I die." And that's the end for them. That's their goal. Their goal is, perversely, implicitly, to die. Because they assume that everything that they do that's valuable is going to end with their death.

This is not the case with Furtwängler. This is not the case with the greatest composers, and the greatest singers. It's not! The purpose is to achieve a quality of immortality, which is not mechanical, which is not a routine, but which creates an image by the performer, by the person who's hearing it, who is experiencing it, to have a premonition of immortality. What's the immortality located in? Well, you're going to die; so what? You're going to die. I've done more living than most, so I can tell you about this.

The importance is what you are doing for the future of mankind. And I can tell you, what Furtwängler did with that Schubert, was exactly impassioned on that basis! He knew he was the end of his culture! Not of his life, but of his culture! And he produced works which he intended to be his signature of immortality. And every human being who really understands what a human being's business is, has the same attitude.

The Meaning of Music

The purpose of life is not to live as long as you can. The purpose of life is to create a future for mankind, just as we're doing now on the question of the galactic water system: The galactic water system principle is now the basis on which the existence of the United States now depends. Because without the application of the galactic water system principle, you cannot save the United States. You cannot save the existence of the United States. It becomes trash. It becomes something which is a dead culture.

And therefore, the purpose of these things, is to give way to the fact of your own actual immortality. Not an immortality you dream about, about your future, but the realization that what you're doing is something which is energizing the immortality of that kind. And that's what we're doing.

Mankind is a unique species! There is nothing like it, there's no animal that's like it. There's no animal which produces mankind. Mankind is a unique phenomenon. And the characteristic of mankind is creativity! And therefore, what you want to do in life, you want to accompany your life with things like great music. Because they perpetuate your existence by perpetuating what you're capable of doing for mankind.

That's why you want to do a good performance, because immortality is looking at you—and raising questions. Here we're talking now about music, but the point is that's what the reason of music is. The meaning is not based on music, it's based on the soul of mankind.

And people who think they're very good at music, actually are mistakenly conceited. They think they conform to a standard, and they probably have conformed to a standard, but it enrages me, because that's not the issue. The great musicians who have the skills will produce the best result required. The rest of us have to experiment, and recognize what we spiritually will accept—and not accept. We are excited by knowing the truth. You don't have to perform the truth, you have to know it.

And I found that most musicians who think they're experts, really are pieces of crap, because they don't know what the meaning of their life is. They don't know what the purpose of their life is; they don't know what the purpose of their music is. And therefore, what they do, they sound acceptable—Hah!—but it's nonetheless crap, because there's no content to the substance there.

The purpose of music is to perfect an insight into beauty, not to produce it. There's too much work to do, to do both at the same time. What you do is you build up a passion, which is a human passion, and which makes music, when it's properly understood, one of the most powerful and important things that mankind can have.

Great Musicians Don't Play Music

The issue is not the sound of the music. That's a mistake. When a musician tries to make the sound of the music, he loses it. Because the practical musician is not a thinker, but more likely a stinker, in my experience. So the problem is, if you don't have a religious motivation in the highest sense of religion, in the sense that you are supposed to be an immortal creature who is going to die—and the immortal creature who is going to die has to transmit something in their life which raises the future of mankind to a higher state. And that's the principle of the matter.

And it's not a Twentieth-Century popular feature. And therefore the Twentieth Century has killed people. They kill their brains, they kill their minds, they kill the

Lyndon LaRouche

EIRNS/Pavel Penev

musician! How do musicians become fartists? Because they went to Twentieth-Century degeneration! We're living in a degenerating culture, and when you try to adapt to a degenerating culture, you destroy the meaning of music!

And you try to be a better musician, and you fail. But if you have a passion for mankind, and if the purpose of music is to enrich your conception of mankind, not some performance in particular. And you find that the greatest musicians compose that way, and perform that way. They don't play music! That's the crap, that's the opportunism. That's the el-cheapo version. What you have to do is, you have to have an embodiment of a mission, an intellectual mission. Which has no notes! But rather, the notes come about as they're dictated to you under that passion. And that's what the great performances are.

Don't try to be a practical musician! That's idiocy! That's the wrong way to go! You should be able to use your instruments. Good! You're able to use your instruments, but where do you go from there? Notes? Bullshit. What you do is you build up a passion, which is a human passion, and which makes music—when it's properly understood—one of the most powerful and important things that mankind can have.

But you really have to absorb it. You think you're smart and that you're a technician. Well, technicians can sometimes pass for musicians. But without passion, without a passion which is independent of any score— how do you pick the score? How do you develop the score? Where's your passion? Is the passion on the sheet? Is it a bunch of notes on a sheet? More likely it's cheap dung, on paper!

We really have to understand what the purpose of this is! Most people are wandering through empty pages, with dung dropped along the way, trying to find in music, a music-per-se solution, in the intention of composition! And that's where the mistake is made. You need a real passion. A fighting passion to reach the truth of mankind. Any musician who seems to be just an ordinary musician of a professional capability—you see today, they're mostly boring people. Their performances are boring. Their interpretations are boring. Routine. Mechanical. And people hide their incompetencies by claiming their technical capabilities. That's a big mistake! You have to have the right passion.

That's why the singer, and the musician performer, but the singer especially, are so important. The singer is extremely important because the singer has one instrument. The mind which controls without his knowing it. That's right! The greatest performers don't know what they're doing—they don't have to! Because they find themselves using a standard of judgment which appeals to a higher authority. They don't want to do something because they don't think it's worth it. They won't change things because they don't think it's right! What's the standard of judgment? The standard of judgment is their sense of immortality.

And what's the purpose of every person's life? You think everybody is supposed to sit around, and get born, and die?! That's not a human function! *The purpose of life is to go beyond the end of it.* And to have contributed to mankind such that mankind would not have achieved otherwise. And every great composer, I guarantee you, every great composer in music operates on that basis, and has operated on that basis. The other guys have tried to fake it. They try to get technical explanations of composition! The technical—that's all part of it—but you've got to fix that thing up! You've got to get rid of the technical stuff. You've got to get into the passion.

And that's what the problem is in politics. The politicians, they're fakers! They're all fakers! They're professionals! Fakers! And it's when you find yourself in the domain of music, or the domain of comparable work, you find yourself carried away by a sense of ob-

EIRNS/Joanne McAndrews

Music is a social process: The Schiller Institute Chorus and Orchestra perform Mozart's Requiem Mass for John F. Kennedy in Boston, Jan. 19, 2014.

ligation to do something which is beyond your apparent will. To reach an effect which seems to you is beyond your ability to willfully create it.

And the most natural thing is the singing voice, the human singing voice. Even the speaking voice, when trained at all, depends upon a creative force. And now when you have to create a sense of the creative force, per se, then all your capabilities as a musician suddenly become real. Whereas, if you try to be a technically perfect musician, it's not so good. Nobody is going to show up for the show. Not for very long. Not twice. Not a few times.

The passion: You live only so long. What makes you a meaningful object for the time before your demise? Are you expressing a passion which is worthy of great musical composition? That's the question.

The Music of the Unheard Performance

Music is a social process, not an individual process. The individual is challenged, but the success is social. And if people would understand that, they would become better musicians. You have to have a driving passion. Just trying to perform something you know is difficult. How do you remember it? Well, you don't remember it, you don't have to. It tells you. It tells you what the score is. It tells you what the performance is.

The passion does it for you.

How did Furtwängler do the Schubert Ninth Symphony? How'd he do it? How does mind work? It's the passion! People who are practical are not really skilled; they're merely trained. And my objective is to get rid of the fakery of perfection, in order to get the skill of art. "Make things beautiful," is a good way of putting it. It's an effect, but it's a good one.

The music lies not in the music. It lies in the motive for the music. Otherwise, what does the music mean? It's just a form of noise-making. You don't want to make noise; you want to capture the mind of people. Not their ears. And the result should come through mind, not through the ears. You interpret the thing not as heard—the "heard sounds."[2] That's what the point is.

What you should hear is the brilliant music of the unheard performance. But you don't have to hear it, because you're already captured by it. You are the property of it. And that's what you have to do if you want to be a good musician. You want to behave as a good musician? You have to be captured by that which you think you're producing, but you're merely a victim of that! Your mind is an instrument. Your body and soul are an instrument of music. It's not the music that makes that. It's the body and soul that makes that. The music is just incidental.

And if it doesn't do that, it doesn't work. You can set out composing all night long, all year long, and you still won't succeed. But if you have the soul for it, it becomes much easier. And how do you do it? By teaching yourself? Not really. By desiring to succeed in teaching how you can, in your own self, generate that which inspires you.

---

2. "Heard melodies are sweet, but those unheard are sweeter..." John Keats, "Ode on a Grecian Urn"

All the usual practical stuff is crap. If you can do it well, that's good. Just don't try to fake it! Let yourself go. Give way to what the meaning of the stuff is. And the meaning is not interpretation; the meaning is something which grips you with a fierce force.

Any singing should be a reflection, at the most, of the intention, the spiritual intention. If it's not there, it's not worth doing. You can make nice sounds—some people do—but they don't convince me. Why don't they convince me? Because I know it's fake.

Music Makes *You*

So now we talk about what Ben has been pushing: the galactic principle![3] Well, the galactic principle happens to be the very basis for the existence of human beings! Not only human beings but a lot of other things which are the collateral pieces of junk which fly around in the system, the galactic system. So everything is on that basis. Kepler always expressed that. Nicholas of Cusa earlier anticipated that same kind of thing. That's mankind! That's the truth of our existence. The practical stuff is shit! It gets in your way. The stink in your nostrils prevents you from seeing things clearly. And everyone really should be able to know that.

But mankind is not an animal. Mankind is not a dog, it's not a cat, it's nothing of the sort. Mankind is a very special kind of creature, which you cannot find by touch, and so forth. And what we're dealing with in the galactic principle is exactly that. All the practical stuff that you're taught is crap! And most of the Twentieth Century is the biggest movement in crap in all of human history!

Anyone who is really honest about music and has any competence knows this. You don't craft it. You don't make it. You give way to it. You're presented with a proposition, an articulation. And once you get the idea, you let yourself go. And the first experiment is awkward because you're not sincere. You're trying to craft something. But you haven't let the object take you over.

Now, people allow things to take them over in the name of music and other things, but that isn't very good. You have to actually understand, you have to create a sense of what humanity's law is, or should be. And you have to find a way that you can give way to express that

kind of law. That's what's crucial. You don't get it by saying, "I'm going to just do it."

My hatred of the crap that I was subjected to in all levels of education, which was the making of me—I never believed in any crap. I never believed in any system. And I was always right on that. Especially in later years. Because people ordinarily today, still today, are degenerating. The Twentieth Century and beyond has been a period of degeneration of mankind. And what we do in music, in working with music from the Eighteenth Century and Nineteenth Century-the problem is that we no longer have any relationship to the Eighteenth and Nineteenth centuries' music. We think we do. We think we can project it, but we don't think that way! We don't believe that way! We don't have a passion that goes that way!

So how can you do music? You make a struggle to imitate yourself, to imitate your own intention. But the creation is different. And we're now at a point which is a great period, because of what Ben has done, in particular, in expostulating this question of the galactic system. The idea of the galactic system is not new. It's old. Kepler already had a very good appreciation in that direction. But the problem is that the Twentieth Century, from the very beginning, was a process of degeneration of humanity. If you were in the Twentieth Century every day of the week, you were becoming worse and worse and worse. That was the general tendency of society.

Look at it! Look at it in terms of physics, physical science. The exact year, the year 1900, defined a degeneration, an increasing degeneration of everything in terms of science and music and culture and everything else. And the only decent things that were produced in music, for example, were things that were spilled over from the Nineteenth Century. The science—the same way. So the point is, unless you realize that you're dealing with an enemy force which is called the Twentieth Century, and now the Twenty-First Century, you are not capable of really understanding what the mission of great music is, because you're so tied to the ties of the standards of the Twentieth and Twenty-First centuries.

And therefore, you really have to walk out of that stage of life, and you have to walk into an area where you can really let yourself go, and express the kinds of things you know you should know. It's true. And it takes a case of a musician, a modern musician, who can survive the crap that's produced generally. It's a question of letting yourself go. Letting yourself go: Just do it!

_____
3. Ben Deniston, "Memo for the Next President: New Perspectives on the Western Water Crisis," *EIR*, April 3, 2015. See also: larouchepac.com/global-water

And then, hearing it, and then having a secret self-criticism, saying, "Who made me do this? What was wrong with it?" And you don't try to say how you can fix it. You have to say, "What was wrong in the total conception of the performance?" Not what was wrong with the part. The so-called part-pleasing thing is crap. It doesn't work, because it's not sincere.

The Principle of Music Is Love

The essential thing is love. Music is love. The principle of music is love, mankind's love of mankind. Of what mankind could be. And you want to do something that's beautiful, in terms of what mankind's nature says. And if it isn't beautiful, you don't want to do it. You don't want ugly things! And the characteristic of the Twentieth Century was ugly music. From the beginning, it's ugly music. And the music has become uglier and uglier and uglier all the time. On every street, even in speaking. In writing. In smelling! In both cases of exhorting, and in-taking.

That's the problem. Mankind tends toward the wrong standards of truth. It starts with the conception that mankind is an animal, and mankind is not an animal. And when you start with saying that mankind is an animal, that's when all the trouble comes in. And the only way you can deal with music, really, is on the basis of love. The love of mankind, and what mankind can do that is loving of mankind.

Because the future is: You're all going to die. And what is the passion which corresponds, therefore, to mankind? Since everybody is going to die, what's the meaning of human life? Is it a fact? Not exactly. It's the creation of a more powerful capability of mankind, by purging mankind of its own corruption. Extracting mankind into the freedom from corruption. And all practical measures to craft and approve a quality of art is crap, because they are not sincere. They don't correspond to some principle of the matter.

And this is true: You see it in drama; you see it on the musical stage; you see it in performance of all kinds.

Franz Schubert

The beauty is creativity, per se. It's also the measure of what creativity is. So you take any composition—it's a sacred business. If you really want to do it, you're attempting a sacred work. And it's a sense of man's immortality. Even people, when they die, if they live well, they can contribute a memory of beauty, and that's rarely done these days.

Now we're in one of the greatest periods, the most emotional part of human history that ever existed. We exist on the brink of the threat of the immediate destruction of the human species by the forces that dominate mankind today. Where do you find the passion that will inform you to take the actions which will save mankind from the destruction which is being brought by mankind on himself, on society? That's music. That's art. It's the sense of immortality, that those people who have died did not die in vain. But what they had decided to do is to commit themselves to the future of mankind.

The beauty of mankind's existence always lies beyond mankind himself. We are able to become the instruments of unleashing the beauty of mankind. Every great composer and every musical performer works on that basis. If they don't do it, they're crap-artists. And I've known a lot of crap-artists.

The Trumpets Have Sounded

Take the case of the Schubert Ninth Symphony. That performance under his direction is a unified piece which contains no separations in the process of delivering the composition. And anyone who does divide it into parts is making an ass of themselves. Because the idea is that you are captured by a transition from one phase to another phase. It's a phase-relationship. It's not a composition of parts of the composition; it's a process of a progressive process. And Schubert, of course, did that!

So you have to understand Schubert in that way. Therefore, you look at Schubert's important works, and all of them have a certain coherence, and what Furtwängler did with his direction of the performance of the Schubert Ninth did exactly that. It's an absolutely perfect composition, which goes from phase to phase to phase without interruption. And when it's delivered that way, it captures the audience—if the audience is sentient—in a way which is unique.

And you just take this, take recordings of the performance of that symphony, and compare them side by side by side. What is unique about what Furtwängler does? Where's the plan? Where's the scheme? Where are the phases? The art, which Schubert himself created, the idea of the perfect composition, which starts from its birth to its completion. There is no interruption, there are no breaks. And the audience is taken from one state of mind, to the next state of mind, to the next state of mind, as a continuous process.

Just think about the finale of that, of how you get into the finale. You go through the whole process, under his direction, the whole process to its completion. And the trumpets have sounded! The trumpets have sounded, and are heard. Why are they heard? And what Furtwängler did in this case was not something exaggerated. It's something which was true. And Furtwängler had the mental power to be able to

do it. It wasn't the orchestra that did it; he did it!

And if you look at him directly, in his direction, you know exactly what he directs. He's relentless. His idea of composition is to drive with an idea, and drive the idea through an evolution, to a conclusion. And that's what we have to do, if we're going to be successful in saving humanity from the kind of crap that's threatening us now. You have to divorce yourself from practicality, and you have to go to the level of genius. Otherwise you won't make it.

You want to do something, you want to move mankind. You don't want to do ordinary things. You don't want to do entertainment. You want to persuade people to become human, which is sometimes a difficult effort.

From the standpoint of the layman, a good performance is magical. And the best audiences in history, in the Twentieth Century, for example, they thought it was magical. The most intelligent musical audiences in that period of time all thought it was magical. It's not magical! It's genius, but that's not magic.

You try to convince people to walk out of the vicissitudes of ordinary life and look at the higher level. What makes life good? What makes living good?

Don't be a musician; be a genius!

The Immortality of Wilhelm Furtwängler

by Matthew Ogden

May 18—Wilhelm Furtwängler died on November 30, 1954. The epitaph which Furtwängler chose for his own tombstone were the words of Saint Paul:

And now abideth Faith, Hope, Love, these three; but the greatest of these is Love.

Not coincidentally, these are also the last words of Johannes Brahms' final vocal composition, *Vier Ernste Gesänge* (*Four Serious Songs*). Brahms' lifelong friend Clara Schumann had suffered a massive stroke in March of 1896, shortly after playing her last public concert, at which she performed Brahms' *Variations on a Theme by Haydn*. Brahms, anticipating that Clara Schumann would soon die, composed this series of four songs based on biblical text. Brahms himself would die the following year.

Brahms asks us: What is the meaning of our lives? Is man nothing more than a beast? Do our lives amount to anything more than the dust which we become? As animals die, so our bodies do as well. Are all of our pleasures, sufferings, trials, aspirations, our experiences between birth and death, nothing greater than mere idle vanities, ephemeral, and lost in time? A breath in the wind? A droplet in the rushing flood?

Or can we see beyond our deaths, as "through a glass, darkly," to something

Wilhelm Furtwängler

which abides after our flesh is gone? To the future, into which the meaning of our lives will persist? As the poet Percy Shelley wrote in verses composed shortly before his own death:

Music, when soft voices die,
Vibrates in the memory…
And so thy thoughts, when thou art gone,
Love itself shall slumber on.

As Wilhelm Furtwängler said of Johannes Brahms in a speech commemorating the centenary of his birth: "Particularly in the last years of his life, he lived with the future, with *eternity*, in mind."

Unheard Melodies

Immortality is not merely the unceasing extension of mortality. It is not a never-ending longevity of the flesh. Rather, just as infinity is not the sum of an unlimited number of finites, *eternity* exists above time, outside of time. The eternal is not contained within, and cannot be attained through the additive aggregate sum of temporals. The sequential chronology of what we call elapsed time is merely the unfolding shadows of something higher—the meaning of each moment cannot be located within the moment itself, but only from the standpoint of the greater flow of which it is a passing part. And without the prior existence of the whole, there could be no possibility for the existence of the parts.

How can we transcend the experience of the moment to participate in the eternal, the universal which created it? How can we be living participants within that whole which supersedes the existence of its subordinate parts?

Just as he said of Brahms, Furtwängler himself lived always "with the future, with eternity, in mind." In fact, the capacity to live in the future—to participate in the eternal—is, in a very real way, the secret that lies behind the almost timeless quality of the experience of a performance by Furtwängler.

The absolutely distinct quality of Furtwängler's performance will immediately grip any sentient listener, and is instantly recognizable. The relentless quality of suspension, a tension always pulling the listener forward from the very beginning through to the very end, an absolute coherence, an unbroken unity—all of these words describe the effect of the almost magical power that Furtwängler commanded over his music and his audiences. The conductor Claudio Abbado describes the effect that even the presence of Furtwängler exerted over his orchestra:

"Even when Furtwängler walked into the pit, there was tension around him—like electricity.... And slowly, this wonderful warm sound came out of the orchestra, and the tension, always this wonderful tension, from beginning to end. He was one of the few musicians who could create tension even in the pauses, when there was nothing but silence."

A seemingly paradoxical idea: a musical tension which exists even in the moments when there is no audible sound. How can there be something in what seems like nothing? For Furtwängler, the notes were not the music, but were merely shadows dancing to a higher music, one that lurks silently but powerfully behind the sensual sounds. As the poet John Keats famously wrote in his *Ode on a Grecian Urn*:

Heard melodies are sweet, but those unheard
Are sweeter; therefore, ye soft pipes, play on;
Not to the sensual ear, but, more endear'd,
Pipe to the spirit ditties of no tone.

This "silent form," which lives outside of time, "dost tease us out of thought as doth eternity." The eerie presence of a ghostly something visiting our present time from beyond time itself is the effect we experience through the music of Furtwängler. We are transported beyond the momentary experience of the part, to an apprehension of the existence of a greater, superior whole, which is constantly exerting its power and control over each passing present moment in time.

Perhaps the most readily available example of this are Furtwängler's recorded performances of Franz Schubert's *Symphony No. 9 in C Major*, the so-called "Great" Symphony. Furtwängler's rendering of this masterpiece remains the standard which no other performance of the work has since achieved. Furtwängler's performance was described by the great Russian conductor Valeri Gergiev in a recent interview, in which he described Furtwängler as a giant, unequaled among all others, the conductor whom he admired most:

"The most difficult thing in conducting is not to slip into mechanical beating. So this restless search for a real tempo, a real pulse, of practically each bar of music, rather than just one tempo for one movement, is something that very few conductors could ever master. Not many conductors will confess, maybe, that it will be something difficult for them to do, but then they will go and compete with Furtwängler, and most probably lose. Because it's a kind of God-given gift, a genius quality, which one conductor contributes to the playing of the orchestra—I describe it in the following: You can't possibly imagine this same orchestra play the way they play with Furtwängler, if you just remove him from the podium. It is just not possible to imagine they will do the same thing. They will be even maybe more organized; they'll be very focused in a certain ensemble; but they will never deliver this kind of incredible expression which he is able to bring to life once being in front of an orchestra....

"Take the example of his performance of the 'Great' Symphony of Franz Schubert.... The quality of symphony and the quality of interpretation. Amazing. I believe in every movement there are so many changes of tempo. First, fantastic theme with horns are playing, and then, in the Second Movement—it seems to be very settled but then it becomes so desperately dramatic. And again, the Third Movement, it's not just going like a clock, you know, da-da-da-da-DA-da-da-da-DA—it has a bite, it has a freedom, it has a fire."

The constant change in tempo so characteristic of Furtwängler's music indicates the presence of a higher law, a higher time, dictating the unfolding of each moment in time. These are not arbitrary changes, not precalculated mathematical values, but the pulse of a living, breathing organism united by a single all-embracing coherent process of development, proceeding always into the future, residing in what is yet to come. The performer subordinates himself to that power, that higher law, striving always toward the apprehension of the unity which brings coherence to the multiplicity of the parts—an almost religious quality of devotion.

Listening to the Future

"Let us consider the activity of artistic creation.... When we look closely at this process, we find we can distinguish two levels. On the first, each individual element combines with those adjacent to it to form larger elements, these larger elements then combining with others and so on, a logical outwards growth from the part to the whole. On the other level, the situation is the reverse: *the given unity of the whole controls the behavior of the individual elements within it, down to the smallest detail.* The essential thing to observe is that in any genuine work of art these two levels complement each other, so that the one only becomes effective when put together with the other....

"The artistic process that has as its starting point the unity of the whole, rests on the concept of a more-or-less complete vision of that whole. For the artist at work, this vision is the goal he seeks to attain; the star that, unbeknownst to him, guides his steps through the maze of obstacles and temptations that beset his path and shows him how to unite the forces at his command. Only at the end of the journey, therefore, will the vision emerge in its totality, not only for the listener, the receiver of the work of art, but also—and this is a vital point—for the composer, the creative artist himself. The total vision only achieves its full radiance when it merges with all the individual sources of light from within the work, the over-all and the particular

Johann Sebastian Bach, in a 1748 portrait by Elias Gottlob Haussmann

interacting and stimulating each other. It is not that the vision is present, ready-made, from the beginning and is only waiting to be filled with artistic substance. On the contrary: the joy that the artist feels comes not from possessing the vision but from the activity of turning it into reality."

—*W. Furtwängler, "Thoughts for All Seasons"*

The foregoing typifies Furtwängler's insight into an actually ontological principle, one which extends far beyond music *per se*, which is as true in science as it is in art. It shouldn't come as a surprise that Furtwängler's contemporaries Max Planck and Albert Einstein were themselves devoted musicians as much as they were scientists. In fact, Furtwängler's composition teacher when he was a young man, Joseph Rheinberger (who was himself a friend and collaborator of Johannes Brahms), had also taught composition to the young Max Planck.

Einstein asserted that the paradoxes pertaining to time and causality presented by Planck's discovery of the quantum would actually be resolved from the standpoint of a higher understanding of music. In an interview published as an appendix to the book *Where Is Science Going?*, Einstein asserted:

"Our present rough way of applying the causal principle is quite superficial.... We are like a juvenile learner at the piano, just relating one note to that which immediately proceed or follows. To an extent this may be very well when one is dealing with very simple and primitive compositions; but it will not do for an interpretation of a Bach Fugue. Quantum physics has presented us with very complex processes, and to meet them, we must further enlarge and refine our concept of causality."

The implications of Einstein's allusion to Bach's fugues are very revealing when considered in light of his contemporary Furtwängler's insights, as quoted above. When we consider the necessary existence of a unified whole in music, which, as Furtwängler says, "controls the behavior of the individual elements within it, down to the smallest detail," we must ask: Where does that whole exist? If the whole cannot exist in any part, nor in the aggregate of all the parts, where and when can we locate the existence of this unifying whole?

Only by *listening to the future*, to that totality which can never exist in the sequential temporal experiences of the ear, but only in the imagination which can consider the entire composition as a one, existing as a unity outside of time. By hearing that single unified Being, and following it as it guides us through the inexorable evolution of its own Becoming. By allowing the inaudible echo of that yet-to-be-experienced future to resonate within the audible sounds of the present, each meeting and mutually interacting with one another at each unfolding moment in time. At no one moment of the sensed experience in time can this whole be perceived; however, it is present at all times, above time, guiding the behavior of each moment of the unfolding experience of time.

Furtwängler expresses this as the intersection between the *Nah-Erleben* and the *Fernhören*, the interaction between "near-experience" with the "distance-hearing," also citing the fugues of Bach as exemplary of the most perfect expression of this principle:

"Bach remains today what he has always been—the divine creator on his throne above the clouds, beyond the reach of others.... Here we find concentration on

Ludwig van Beethoven, by Joseph Karl Stieler, 1820

the moment in time united with the unheard expanse; the immediate realization of the part paired with the truly sovereign overall vision of the whole. With its ever-conscious feeling for the near and the far at the same time; with its unconstrained fulfillment of the here-and-now joined with an ever-present subconscious feeling for the structure, the current of the whole; its 'near-experience' [*Nah-Erleben*] with its 'distance-hearing' [*Fernhören*], Bach's music is a greater example of biological certainty of purpose and natural power than we will find anywhere else in Music. Precisely this is what makes Bach's music so truly unique.... Bach, the creator of these choruses and these fugues, seems to be not a human being, but the spirit that rules the world, the very architect of the universe.... It is this that makes him for us the greatest of all composers, the Homer of music, whose light still shines out across our musical firmament, and whom, in a very special sense, we have never surpassed."

—W. Furtwängler, "Bach"

In Bach, we experience at every moment this intersection of the near with the far, the part with the whole, the microcosm with the macrocosm, the temporal with the eternal. As Furtwängler describes elsewhere, the mission of the artist is always to seek: "the fulfillment of the moment within a larger process. Each individual thing has its own function and this within the development of the whole. The two meet and intersect at each moment. It is not always easy at first to grasp the fact that every detail has its function within the whole, and is not only 'arranged' within this whole, but often has an effect on the whole that goes far beyond its individual importance.... This single-mindedness of purpose, this clear and unmis-

takable cohesion of the whole can only be created through real laws, based in nature."
—*W. Furtwängler, "Notebooks," 1946*

'If I Have Not Love, I Am Nothing'

"Love—love that is forever being seized and shaken by the work—can never be replaced. Love alone creates the preconditions for the visionary and correct understanding of 'the whole' in the work of art, for *this whole is nothing but love.* Each individual part can be more or less understood intellectually, but the whole can only ever be grasped by *the living feeling of love.* It is the only thing which is appropriate and fitting to the whole work of art as an image of the active and living world. Everything else, however skillful it may be, is limited, and therefore profoundly boring to me."
—*W. Furtwängler, "Notebooks," 1936*

As the 19th Century drew to a close, Johannes Brahms' setting in his *Four Serious Songs* of the words of St. Paul speaks almost as a prophesy, a warning to musicians, a eulogy for art in the century to come:

"Though I speak with the tongues of men and of angels, and have not love, I am become as sounding brass, or a tinkling cymbal."

St. Paul at his writing desk, by Rembrandt van Rijn, 1629

As Furtwängler insisted, without the dedication to the "the living feeling of love" which is required to grasp the understanding of a work of art in its wholeness, music dies, and becomes nothing more than the intellectualized assembly of individual separate parts rather than a single, living, organic whole. In the essay cited previously, Furtwängler asks the question: what is the emotion which is required by the artist to grasp this fundamental unity of the whole?

"Corresponding to the power that works inwards, from the whole to the parts, a power which proceeds from a more or less complete vision of the whole, is an emotion that springs from the artist's relationship to the world at its most profound and most meaningful—an emotion one may call love, humility, reverence, worship, awe, and many other things ... a love of the world, which comes to us as the eternal gift of God. If only modern man would grasp that it is impossible to understand and shape the world as it confronts us without loving it! And that it is equally impossible to love it

without seeking, in the context of this love, to understand it!"

For Furtwängler, the late compositions of Beethoven represented the high-point in this ideal of cohesive artistic unity in which the parts became absolutely subordinated and inseparable from the whole—an ideal which, however, was increasingly abandoned following Beethoven's death.

"With Beethoven, the parts increasingly lost their independence, to the point where they were incomprehensible without reference to the whole; no part made sense without reference to that which preceded it and that which followed. Up to the time of Beethoven, musical development had taken place with the tacit assumption that the work of art emerged like an organism.... Whereas Beethoven sought to bring out the whole with ever greater clarity and power, his contemporaries, but even more his successors, turned away from this approach, and the concept of the work of art as an organic whole crumbled in their hands...."

The irony, however, of the rejection of the concept of the organic whole, is that, since the very existence of the parts depends upon the existence of the whole, in the absence of this whole, there also ceases to be the possibility of the parts!

"Today the concept of overall form has lost its central, dominant position. No longer does it appear to be able to assert itself over the material. *No longer is it the whole that controls the behavior of the parts....* The whole has been consumed by the parts, with the result that, not only is there no longer a whole, but there are also no longer any parts, because these can only exist so long as there is a whole to which they can refer! Everything exhausts itself in the individual moment, no heed being paid either to what has gone before or to what follows. The consequence is a concentration on the effect of the moment, effect for its own sake, in harmony, in rhythm, in orchestration, and through numerous little titillating details."

Thus, quite literally: "Though I speak with the tongues of men and of angels, and have not love, I am become as sounding brass, or a tinkling cymbal." Furtwängler clearly identified what he saw as the tragedy of music's decline as being fundamentally rooted in the loss among his contemporaries of the capacity for love.

"Our only hope of salvation, a return to the inspiration that comes from the living masterpieces of music, is all-too-often stultified by bad performances. The inability to feel the fundamental emotional content of a work through its entire course, from beginning to end, is at its most glaringly obvious in those works of whose living example we stand in greatest need today. It is those works that receive the worst performances because they are the very ones that make the greatest spiritual demands on the performer."

The Music of Our Soul

Pope Francis recently stated in an interview, that for him, the most "Promethean" of all conductors is Wilhelm Furtwängler, citing Furtwängler's performances of Beethoven, and especially Bach, specifically his *St. Matthew's Passion*, saying: "The piece by Bach that I love so much is the 'Erbarme Dich,' the tears of Peter in the *St. Matthew's Passion*. Sublime."

And indeed, Furtwängler's music has a reverential, devout, almost religious quality to it. The orchestra under Furtwängler, becomes fused into a single instrument, a single organism, and becomes in his words "a point of entry of the divine."

"The sense of the orchestra as an artistic medium is that this body, constituting of 90-100 different people, different heads and hands, becomes one instrument through which a soul, a feeling, an intuition is communicated to the listener in its tiniest details. The more it achieves this, the more it loses its vanity of wanting to be something itself, the more it becomes the mediator, the communicator, the vessel and point of entry of the divine, speaking through the great masters."
—*W. Furtwängler, "Notebooks," 1929*

Furtwängler sought to transport his audiences from the mere temporal experience of the passing moment and into the universal, the eternal, the whole. This becomes the almost sacred devotion of the true artist and the true scientist alike. As Albert Einstein wrote in 1930, in an article published in the *New York Times Magazine*, describing what he called the "cosmic religious feeling" which motivates the great scientist:

"The individual feels the futility of human desires and aims, and the sublimity and marvelous order which reveal themselves both in nature and in the world of thought. Individual existence impresses him as a sort of prison and he wants to *experience the universe as a single significant whole*. How can this cosmic religious feeling be communicated from one person to another … ? In my view, it is the most important function of art and science to awaken this feeling and keep it alive in those who are receptive to it."

Furtwängler's music allows us to do just that. Furtwängler enables his audiences to escape that prison of shadows and sense-experience, and to experience instead the *unheard* music which lies beyond the notes. Each sound may quickly die, but the music which created it is eternal.

As Furtwängler's great friend and collaborator, the violinist Yehudi Menuhin said:

"There are many conductors, but very few of them seem to reveal that secret chapel that lies at the very heart of all masterpieces. Beyond the notes, there are visions, and beyond those visions, there is this invisible and silent chapel, where an inner music plays, the music of our soul, whose echoes are but pale shadows. That was the genius of Furtwängler because he approached every work like a pilgrim who strives to experience this state of being that reminds us of Creation, the mystery which is at the heart of every cell. With his fluid hand movements, so full of meaning, he took his orchestras and his soloists to this sacred place."

Mathematical Economics: A Satanic Religion

by Robert Ingraham

An earlier version of this article appeared in the July 27, 2007 EIR.

May 18—In 1956, an engineer at Bell Labs in Murray Hill, N.J. published, in the *Bell System Technical Journal*, an article titled, "A New Interpretation of Information Rate." The engineer's name was John Kelly, and the article, which was prepared with the help of another Bell engineer, Claude Shannon—famous today as one of the founders of Information Theory—posed the question of whether a mathematical formula could be devised to ensure success in betting on horse races. Kelly answered the question in the affirmative, and his solution, the "Kelly Formula" or "Kelly Criterion," not only became the basis for several gambling systems in Las Vegas and Atlantic City, but is also widely used today in financial options trading, where it is sometimes called the "Geometric Mean Maximizing Portfolio Strategy." Use of the Kelly method, according to one options-trading authority, is intended to "maximize the value of the logarithm of wealth."

In 1960, Claude Shannon introduced the Kelly Formula to Edward Thorp, a mathematics professor at MIT. Beginning in 1960, using an IBM Fortran 740 mainframe computer at MIT, Thorp programmed a statistical computer program to win at blackjack. In 1960 and 1961, Shannon and Thorp took several trips to Las Vegas to test their theories on blackjack and roulette. Subse-

From blackjack to "new financial instruments"

quently, Thorp presented his blackjack system in a paper, "Fortune's Formula," to the annual conference of the American Mathematical Association. Then, in 1962, Thorp issued a public challenge to casino owners that he could beat their games, traveled to Reno, Nev., and in two days, doubled his money playing blackjack. Later that year, Thorp published a more popularized version of his method and experiences in the best-selling book *Beat the Dealer*.

Shortly after these events, Edward Thorp relocated to the University of California at Irvine, and began to investigate how to use his winning blackjack strategy to make money in financial investments. During the next ten years, he became one of the pioneers in the emerging field of "new financial instruments," particularly after the opening of the Chicago Board of Options Exchange in 1973.

In 1967, Thorp published a book on investment strategy titled *Beat the Market: A Scientific Stock Market System*. In this work he presented the first, basic version of what would be later known as the famous *Black-Scholes Formula*. In 1969, Thorp opened Convertible Hedge Associates, described as the world's first market-neutral hedge fund. Later renamed Princeton Newport Partners (PNP), this hedge fund flourished until 1988, when it was raided and shut down as part of the U.S. government's racketeering case against Michael Milken/Drexel Burnham. Thorp survived, creating a new hedge fund, Edward O. Thorp and Associates, in Newport Beach, Calif., which exists to this day.

In 1973, Thorp received a letter from Fisher Black, in which Black expressed his admiration for Thorp's work. Black included in the letter a copy of the Black-Scholes Formula, which was about to be published. This letter began a friendship between Thorp and Black which lasted until the latter's death in 1995. Later that year, Thorp presented a paper, "Extensions of the Black-Scholes Option Model," at the annual conference of the International Statistical Institute in Vienna.

Through the 1970s and '80s, Thorp continued to play a leading role in the initiation of new financial investment methods. In 1974, he developed the first mathematical solution to the American "put curve."[1] In 1979, Thorp and his team at PNP came up with the idea of "statistical arbitrage." According to Thorp, their intent was to "use the Brownian motion structure of stock prices to 'drain energy' [i.e., money] from the ceaselessly excessive fluctuations in stock prices."

Thorp is still very much active today. In 1997, he presented a paper, "The Kelly Criterion in Blackjack, Sports Betting, and the Stock Market," to the Tenth International Conference on Gambling and Risk Taking, in Montreal; and, in 2003, the *Quantitative Finance Review* published a piece by him, titled "A Perspective on Quantitative Finance: Models for Beating the Market."

During these last several decades Thorp's writings have moved back and forth seamlessly between the worlds of gambling and "mathematical economics," with a unity of approach that spans both.

Going Further

• At a 1963 conference on computer science, held in Las Vegas, computer programer Harvey Dubner proposed a revision to the Thorp blackjack system, utilizing a method based on a "high-low" card count. Another computer programmer, Julian Braun, then played over 90 million simulated blackjack hands on an IBM 7044 computer until he had perfected Dubner's revisions to the Thorp system. Braun was an IBM engineer, with degrees in mathematics and physics. After leaving IBM in 1987, he became a day-trader in stocks and commodities. In 1967, a revised version of *Beat the Dealer*, including the Thorp/Braun combined method, was published. This work has remained the basis for all blackjack winning strategies down to the present day.

• The final development in successful blackjack strategy was the invention of team play, first by Ken Uston in the 1970s, and then, more spectacularly, by the MIT blackjack team in the 1990s. Uston, a magna cum laude graduate of Yale University, with an MBA from Harvard, was, by 1967, the vice-president of the Pacific Stock Exchange in San Francisco. He quit his job to take up blackjack full-time. He was the first to utilize team play, which he described in his 1977 book, *The Big Player*. In the 1990s a group of MIT mathematics and physics undergraduates created the "MIT Blackjack Club," and, using a method which combined the Thorp/Braun betting system and Uston's team strategy, over a period of several years won millions of dollars from the Las Vegas casinos. Their exploits were described in the 2002 book *Bringing Down the House—The Inside Story of Six MIT Students Who Took Vegas for Millions*.

One last figure in the field of blackjack worth mentioning is John Ferguson (a.k.a. Stanford Wong), who refined many of the betting methods of Thorp, Braun, and Uston. Ferguson, who holds a Ph.D. in economics from Stanford University, published *Professional Blackjack* in 1975, which to this day is considered the all-around best book on the topic.

• In 2001, Texas banker Andrew Beal traveled to Las Vegas for the express purpose of defeating the best professional poker players in the world. Beal's efforts, which continued for several years, are chronicled in the popular 2005 book *The Professor, the Banker and the Suicide King: Inside the Richest Poker Game of All Time*, by Michael Craig. Beal is the founder and president of the Dallas-based Beal Bank, which he created in 1988 on the wreckage of the Texas savings and loan industry. During the past 20 years, his bank has specialized in buying and selling "distressed properties," and, among other "investments," it provided some of the financial backing for Enron Corp. to move into the deregulated California energy market. By his own account, Beal spent thousands of hours writing and running computer programs in order to perfect a winning poker strategy. His poker games in Las Vegas still hold the record as the biggest high-stakes games of all time, where, in some games, there was as much as $30 million on the table. Beal is also an amateur mathematician and student of number theory. In 1997, the American Mathematical Society published a paper by Beal, "Beal's Conjecture," which purported to contain a solution to Fermat's Last Theorem.

• In 1981, a group of physics and mathematic stu-

---

1. In options trading, there are two types of contracts: 1) an option to buy a commodity at a future date, known as a "call" option, and, 2) an option to sell a commodity at a future date, known as a "put" option.

dents at the University of California at Santa Cruz formed a club named the Dynamical Systems Collective, but popularly called the Chaos Club. They studied chaos theory, played around with fractals, and decided to devise a method to win money at the roulette tables in Las Vegas. Their adventures were recounted in the 2000 book *The Eudaemonic Pie*, by Thomas A. Bass. Later, in 1992, the same group of now ex-students founded an investment firm, The Prediction Company, in Sante Fe, N.M. The idea for the company grew out of a series of conferences held between 1986 and 1991, where arguments centered around the view that financial markets were essentially stochastic[2] in nature, and that chaos theory provided the basis for predicting safe bets in chosen financial instruments. The seed money to create The Prediction Company came from David Weinberger, who began his career at Bell Labs, and went on to become a bond trader at Goldman Sachs. When Weinberger left Goldman Sachs, he was replaced by none other than Fisher Black, of Black-Scholes fame.

Between 1975 and 1985, the Black-Scholes methodology revolutionized finance—Everyone adopted it. Earlier, in 1969, Myron Scholes had created new financial strategies which led to the development of hedge funds and index funds. In 1973, the Black-Scholes Formula was published in the *Journal of Political Economy*. The formula assumes that stock prices follow a "geometric Brownian motion with constant volatility." In 1973, the Chicago Board of Options Exchange opened options trading, based on the work of Black and others.

In 1985, while working for Goldman Sachs, Fisher Black developed the "Black-Derman-Toy" model, which led to the rapid expansion of the derivatives market. Perhaps the most important figure in this circle, however, was neither Black nor Scholes, but their friend and collaborator, Robert Merton. Merton received a Ph.D. in economics from MIT in 1970. In 1973, he published "The Theory of Rational Options Pricing," in the *Bell Journal of Economics and Management*. Merton proposed a "stochastic calculus," which, according to him, allowed the behavior of option prices to be described in the language of classic probability theory. Merton went on to work at Solomon Brothers, and then became a managing director at J.P. Morgan. He is often credited with opening the doors at Wall Street banking and investment firms for mathematics professors. In

1997, Merton and Scholes were awarded the Nobel Prize in Economics.

Self-evidently, each one of these math nerds was a compulsive gambler. But—what is compulsive gambling? It is nothing but obsessive, continual, uninterrupted worship of Satan—or some equivalent devil. When dice are thrown into the air or dropped (or when a deck of cards is shuffled for a "game of chance," or whenever you reach out to draw a card in such a game), you are delivering those dice, just momentarily, into the hands of an all-powerful demon (known in mathematical physics as "Maxwell's Demon"). With his uncanny powers, that one fleeting moment of opportunity is more than enough for him. Working his will within a fraction of the wink of an eye, he subtly gives the dice a tiny extra spin as they shoot through the air, causing them to drop into a pattern which has a predetermined, unique meaning for you—for you, the compulsive gambler.

Gypsies tell fortunes through "random" drawings of Tarot cards, and through the random results of the throw of special, magical dice. But the compulsive gambler uses what appear (to you) to be ordinary dice, ordinary cards, and many other objects and events to the same effect. And always in deadly earnest.

Indeed—what is random? What is Randomness? Randomness itself, personified, is the object of worship for statisticians and other sorts of mathematical quasi-zombies.

The 20th-Century Austrian-American psychoanalyst Edmund Bergler, who treated compulsive gamblers with some success, wrote a famous article and a book about them, and generally pioneered this subject. Bergler rightly taught that the compulsive gambler is in a "rebellion against reason." But there is more to it even than that; what he calls a "rebellion against reason," would more truthfully be described as the rebellion of Milton's Satan against God. Other psychoanalysts speak of a stage of development in which the infant conceives of his mother as an all-powerful witch, and of himself as her sorcerer. Saturated as it is with Satanism and magic, that pattern resonates with the facts of compulsive gambling.

But the great artists have picked up the trail where the psychoanalyst Bergler left it. Read Pushkin's "Queen of Spades," and Edgar Allan Poe's "Le Duc De l'Omelette," and "Never Bet the Devil Your Head," among others. Learn to recognize and shun that sulphurous smell before you end up like the Mathematical Economists yourself.

---

2. I.e., random or aimless.

The Study of Life and The New Physics

by Vladimir I. Vernadsky

1930 Conference of the Society of Naturalists of Moscow and Leningrad

Translated from French by Meghan Rouillard

Translator's Introduction[1]

In this revolutionary piece, published in 1930 in French in the Revue des Sciences, Vladimir Vernadsky makes a powerful and provocative argument for the need to develop what he calls "a new physics," something he felt was clearly necessitated by the implications of the groundbreaking work of Louis Pasteur among few others, but also something which was required to free science from the long-lasting effects of the work of Isaac Newton, most notably.

For hundreds of years, science had developed in a direction which became increasingly detached from the breakthroughs made in the study of life and the natural sciences, detached even from human life itself, and committed reductionists and small-minded scientists were resolved to the fact that ultimately all would be reduced to "the old physics." The scientific revolution of Ein-

Vladimir Ivanovich Vernadsky
(1863–1945)

stein was a step in the right direction, but here Vernadsky insists that there is more progress to be made. He makes a bold call for a new physics, taking into account and fundamentally based upon the striking anomalies of life and human life.

I.

The revolution which in our 20th century is taking place in physics, raises, for scientific thought, the necessity of a new revision of fundamental biological representations. It seems that for the first time it is becoming possible, in the cosmos constructed by science, to promote the phenomena of life to an important place. It is for the first time in the course of three centuries that the possibility of overcoming the profound contradictions created by the historic progress of thought is opening to us: contradictions between the scientifically constructed cosmos and the life of humanity; between the conception of the surrounding world connected with the conscience of man and its scientific expression. This contradiction has penetrated our intellectual life since the 16th century; we

---

1. Footnotes are translator's footnotes, unless otherwise indicated. The relatively smaller number of footnotes presumably by Vernadsky from the 1930 French edition will be indicated by brackets. Italics reflect the original document unless otherwise indicated.

feel it profoundly with each step. Its consequences are innumerable.

It is therefore important to follow attentively and to contemplate the development of the new physics, as the changes produced in our life due to the creation of the new scientific picture of the Cosmos—a consequence of the new physics—in which the contradiction with the human sentiment will not exist, these changes grow with the progress of physics.

This revolution must have no less of an impact upon the essential instrument of scientific thought—everyday scientific work, the psychology of researchers, because it has created, as we will see, a striking unconformity in the course of recent centuries between the scientific picture of the world and the scientific work upon which it is based.

Thus we are witnessing one of the greatest processes in the progress of scientific thought, and one of the age-old crises of human consciousness.

II.

Our scientific picture of the cosmos has its genesis at the time of the Renaissance. In the 16th Century, Giordano Bruno (1548–1600) clearly expressed the infinity of the universe and the small place occupied by our Sun, not to the mention the Earth.[2] Nicholas of Cusa (1401–1464) had understood this and expressed it one century before him.[3] Bruno said, with greater clarity than others, something which, in that time, was raised in all areas of human consciousness. In fact, the construction of Bruno was not a scientific acquisition, but he drew unprecedented philosophical conclusions from new scientific discoveries, conclusions which surpassed that which was scientifically known, and which were in agreement with the later development of scientific understanding. The entire scientific conception of the universe changed in a radical way. The tradition of thousands of years was shattered.

The philosophical constructions deduced from new facts and scientific empirical generalizations got ahead of the later acquisitions of precise scientific thought by several generations.

Based upon the telescope, a new conception, a new scientific sense of the Universe[4] developed in the course of a small number of generations: in the course of several decades, Copernicus, Kepler, Galileo, and Newton shattered the age-old relationship that had been formed between man and the universe.

The scientific picture of the Universe, embraced by the laws of Newton, left no room for any manifestation of life, despite its appearing to have reached the limits of scientific perfection.

Not only man, not only life, but our entire planet gets lost in the infinity of the Cosmos. Up to now, man and, through him, the phenomena of life, occupied a central place in the Cosmos, in the scientific, philosophical, religious and artistic constructions; at the end of the 17th century all of these representations disappeared from the scientific concepts about the Universe.

Ascribing excessive dimensions to the world, the new scientific concept of the Universe seemed, at the same time, to belittle man with his interests and conquests, to belittle all the phenomena of life, to the point of being a species of insignificant detail in the Cosmos.

It seemed that the more human thought developed, the more such a scientifically constructed Cosmos, totally foreign and inconceivable to all that lived, to every human personality and to human life, emerged with more vigor and clarity.

After Newton, this picture of the Universe, devoid of life, penetrated by scientific thought, more quickly established itself outside of any philosophical or religious representations, due to the scientific observation of surrounding nature.

Its importance was especially developed during the periods of great success of stellar astronomy.

The first of these epochs came at the turn of the 19th century, the time of William Herschel and his sister Caroline Herschel, who discovered a new world and demonstrated for the first time the regularity of its construction, in particular the existence of an infinite number of nebulae, of stellar cosmic systems.

We are now living through the second epoch, in the 20th century. The new blossoming of stellar astronomy is in large part due, on the one hand to powerful new

---

2. Bruno, tried for heresy in 1593 by the Roman Inquisition, had posited that stars were suns with their own exoplanets, and that they could potentially harbor life. Vernadsky's particular reference here is to his insistence that the universe was infinite, and had no body at its center. To quote Bruno: "The universe is then one, infinite, immobile.... It is not capable of comprehension and therefore is endless and limitless, and to that extent infinite and indeterminable, and consequently immobile."

3. It should be noted that this reference to Cusa does not appear in the Russian Academy of Sciences publication of this piece.

4. Capitalization is consistent with the original. This may vary throughout in the case of Universe, Cosmos, etc..

Nicholas of Cusa (1401–1464), founder of modern science and leading organizer of the Renaissance, whom Vernadsky describes elsewhere as "one of the most original and prodigious minds of his time."

methods of observation developed with an unprecedented momentum by the American observatories, and on the other hand to the immediate adoption of scientific observations by physics. The new astrophysical discoveries penetrate the new physics and are more and more guided by its constructions.

This is where the radical distinction of the new progress of stellar astronomy from those of the earlier scientific generalizations lies, from that of Hipparchus, Ptolemy, Brahe, the Herschels and the Struves.[5]

Within the scientific milieu and that of learned men, in the 18th and 20th centuries, voices were immediately and unceasingly raised, which indicated with concern the futility of life, as well as all other great human desires, a futility which seemed to result from the grandi-

ose picture of the Cosmos. These spiritual[6] and intellectual tendencies found their justification in the cosmogonies based upon these observations. The English astronomer M. Jeans presented them again recently in his speeches which drew the attention of the entire world. The fragility and the insignificance of life, its accidental nature in the Cosmos, always seems to find new confirmations due to the progress of exact science.

But this new development of the scientific picture of the Universe, established in the framework of scientific thought, will today intersect for the first time another, more profound current of conception of the world, which changed the empirically obtained picture of the Cosmos in a radical way.

It is neither philosophical analysis, nor religious sentiment, but scientific thought which begins to introduce corrections, to shed light, in a new way, upon the scientific picture of the Cosmos, considered for a long time as a stranger to human life.

Based upon generalizations and astrophysical theories this picture changes, unexpectedly for contemporaries, thanks to the influence of the profound revolution which the fundamental constructions of physics have undergone.

A new wave in the new scientific structure of the Universe is rising. It puts these burning contradictions which have existed for centuries into a new framework.

III.

Until now, man could only resolve the contradictions which existed between his own conception of the world, and that of the scientific picture, by addressing it through either philosophy or religion.

Over the course of many centuries, the scientist had not reconciled the fact that neither he, nor any living thing—consciousness, thought, intelligence—all there is which is higher for him, could in any way impact the scientific picture of the Cosmos, nor introduce corrections in the construction of the Cosmos,—created by science, except by borrowing from other domains of the spiritual life of humanity, that of philosophy, religion, and in part, art.

Remaining on the ground of the scientific concep-

---

5. The Struve family was a dynasty of five generations of astronomers from the 18th–20th centuries in Germany and Russia, including most notably Friedrich Georg Wilhelm von Struve, who worked on problems such as double stars, Otto Wilhelm von Struve, who headed the Pulkovo Observatory, and his descendants, Ludwig Struve, Hermann Struve, Georg Otto Hermann Struve, and Otto Struve.

6. Vernadsky used the adjectives *"spirituel"* in the French and *"dukhovny"* in the Russian versions of this article. Their sense is often broader than most modern English usage of "spiritual," encompassing what English conveys by "mental," "intellectual," or "of the mind," as well. Henceforth this will be translated simply as "spiritual."

tion, he had to accept the scientific picture of the Cosmos, foreign to life, and to treat as an error and an illusion the importance which he always gave in life to intelligence and consciousness, to all living things of which he himself was a part.

Faced with the impossibility of actually scientifically reducing of phenomena of life to physico-chemical phenomena, taking as a basis the picture of the Cosmos of recent times, he brought about a great movement in the scientific environment and that of educated men, which proclaimed that sooner or later it would be done, without radically changing the founding principles which were considered as unshakeable.

It was estimated that intelligence, consciousness, the most elevated properties of life, should be able to be reduced, along with all the other physiological processes, to physico-chemical processes which are a part of the structure of the Cosmos. It was thought that all philosophical, artistic and religious manifestations of human consciousness would be included in Newton's scientific framework of the Universe without exception.

Philosophical thought never reconciled itself with such a representation: the analysis of philosophers and a great number of scientists who had reflected on the founding principles of their knowledge had arrived at the conclusion that this representation did not flow from scientific knowledge, and that [belief in this reduction and inclusion][7] was essentially nothing but faith, which was based on philosophical and even metaphysical representations.

Philosophical admissions, foreign to the exact sciences, constitute the basis of another tentative scientific explanation, having as its objective to become the master of contradictions, the acceptance of forces or forms of energy or of entelechy specific to the phenomena of life, foreign to the inanimate world.

These vitalist representations were not able to enter into scientific thought in a lasting way, as their roots are not found in exact and empirical material of scientific generalizations and facts, but were introduced into science by constructions and foreign philosophical research.

Based only on the analysis of the fundamental content of science, scientific facts and the generalizations deduced from them, and relying only upon them, the scientist was forced to admit that there was not a real

basis for the belief that the physico-chemical phenomena of Newton's picture of the Universe were sufficiently profound and vast to embrace all the phenomena of life, and that at the same time it was impossible to deduce from them, from their empirical material, vitalist representations which would have completed the picture of the Universe.

Aside from the logical analysis of scientific knowledge and the scientifically constructed universe, it is the observation of the history of scientific knowledge of recent centuries which had to give him this conviction.

In reality, the explanation of life given by the models of the dominant conception of the scientific universe has not made progress in the course of recent centuries. The same abyss stands between living matter and non-living, abiotic matter, as during the time of Newton.

The models and the constructions of physico-chemical systems of the Cosmos of Newton have not, up to this point, succeeded in scientifically explaining consciousness, intelligence, and logical thought.

The scientist had to search for a way out of these contradictions, either in philosophical or religious thought, or in the reconstruction of the scientific Universe, in which the phenomena of life expressed in scientific facts and empirical generalizations had to be included, along with other manifestations of reality.

IV.

Despite the generally widespread conviction of the immutability of the modern scientific representation of the Universe, despite its very enhanced precision in the last century, this representation did not acquire, in its basic principles, either the sufficient resilience or authority such that the place which life found there could be considered as proven, and that the scientist, remaining only on the ground of scientific knowledge, had to swallow his pride, to submit to and recognize the futility and the insignificance of life in the Cosmos.

Religious and philosophical thought gave an entirely different place to life in the Universe. Philosophical research developed quickly in the course of three centuries (and what a development it was!) in the opposite direction to that of the scientific picture of the world, while the religious constructions incessantly changed the elements which collided with scientific thought.

The awareness of the phenomena of life and their immense importance in the Cosmos was simultane-

---

7. Added for sake of clarity.

ously deepened in philosophy, in religious creation and in the life of humanity.

The evolution of scientific thought, in this spiritual environment, little by little, and imperceptibly for contemporaries, ate away at the belief in the possibility of including the phenomena of life in the scientific picture of the universe without radically changing it.

But there is more. The change in this direction was inevitably prepared for a new phenomenon—the development and the structure of the scientific organization of humanity.

This is a matter of what follows.

With the progress of scientific work, after the brilliant success brought to the 18th and 19th Centuries by the descriptive natural sciences, and the penetration of precise scientific methods in the domain of the humanitarian sciences in the same centuries, the place occupied by the scientific picture of the Cosmos in scientific knowledge continuously decreased. Indeed, the scientific picture of the Cosmos was only completed by an ever-shrinking number of scientific researchers. An ever-growing part of the persistent work of humanity lost its connection with the scientifically created picture of the Universe.

The face of science has been completely transformed in the course of these two and a half centuries which followed the Principles of Natural Philosophy of Newton; entire sciences were created which had not existed during that time, and the overwhelming mass of these new sciences is related to the study of life and of humanity in particular.

It is not to be doubted that well over nine out of ten of all scientists work in domains of science which have no connection with the picture of the Cosmos, falsely considered to be a result of scientific work as a whole.

They are not at all interested in this picture and do not encounter it in the course of any of their scientific activity. Its change does not arise in the domain of their knowledge. They completely pass over it.[8]

This is demonstrated in a striking way in the history of the biological sciences of the 19th Century for example. The theory of the evolution of species which still plays such an important role in the conceptions of the last 70 years, and in the entire life of humanity, doesn't enter into the scientific picture of the Cosmos, since life is not represented there.

The history of the theory of evolution has not yet been written from this point of view but it is very curious and produces a completely different effect upon us today which it did not have at the time upon the people who had been a part of its creation. It animated the cosmogonic evolutionary representations, but finds itself in strong opposition to the physico-chemical researches of biology. Its agreement with the Cosmos of Newton, that is, the possibility of completely reducing it to the physico-chemical principles forming the basis of the Cosmos, always seemed doubtful: perhaps more doubtful at the time of C. Darwin than in the period that followed. In all cases it exerted a large influence upon scientific thought and did not figure into the scientific picture of the Universe.

We are now at a turning point. It is possible that the unconscious progress of scientific thought of the last decades moved in a direction which has destroyed the belief in the possibility of reducing the phenomena of life to the parameters of the Cosmos of Newton.

V.

The ground was therefore prepared unconsciously in the psychology of scientific workers, in part by following the progress of the theory of evolution, as we will now see.

Science is not an abstract entity, self-sufficient, with an independent existence. It is a creation of human life and exists only within this life. Its content is not limited by scientific theories, by hypotheses, or by models of the picture of the universe created by them. This content is principally made up of scientific facts and their empirical generalizations. The real content of science is the scientific work of living individuals.

These living individuals, scientific workers, constitute science as a social phenomenon: their spiritual dis-

---

8. The problem of over-specialization in science was something a young Vernadsky struggled with. In 1896, he wrote: *"I feel that I am becoming a specialist, part of my interests are receding and although along with this the intensity of the work in a specialized area is strengthened[,] this is connected with a well known narrowing of the mind. In this respect my expedition to the Urals [which he was then visiting with his students] has done much for me and two roads have clearly opened before me—one, although little productive and partly dilettantism, at the same time forces the mind to work more intensely and more broadly, the other is more productive, more defined—but at the same time confines the mind within the specific parameters and inevitably shrinks the*

horizon, placing a person within the ranks of scientific workers but not among the creators of the unfolding process." (Bailes, Kendall, "Science and Russian Culture in An Age of Revolutions: V.I. Vernadsky and His Scientific School, 1863–1945," Indiana University Press, 1990, p. 68.)

Sir Isaac Newton (1642–1726), who sought to reduce all phenomena in the universe to a set of physico-chemical processes, which, according to Vernadsky, "left no room for any manifestation of life" nor could they be successful "in scientifically explaining consciousness, intelligence, and logical thought." Vernadsky therefore demands that science be liberated from the reductionist beliefs of Isaac Newton and that a "new physics" and a "new scientific picture of the Cosmos" be established on the basis of the study of life and human life (1702 portrait by Godfrey Keller).

position, their mastery, the level of their understanding and their satisfaction with the work they have accomplished, their will—this global scientific viewpoint—are essential factors in the historic progress of scientific knowledge.

Science is a complex social creation of humanity, unique and incomparable to anything else, it has a much more universal character than literature or art, and has little relationship to the forms of life of the state and society. It is a global social formation, as the forces of facts and generalizations, equally obligatory for the entire world, form its base.

There exists nothing comparable in any other spiritual domain of human life.

Science is made up of living personalities, bound by this universal obligation. This is why it is by no means a matter of indifference if the fundamental theoretical

results of their work are foreign to and have no relation with the scientific *work* of the overwhelming number of living personalities and thinkers who represent science.[9]

We are seeing this in the current period. The content of scientific work is, for the most part, not even reflected in the scientific picture of nature.

This can only continue because of a belief that the scientific work of scientists will end up being bound by the current scientific picture of the universe and will not contradict it; this faith still persists. Many people are expecting it, occupying themselves with their special work, and are not concerned about the future.

If the faith disappears, the contradiction between the content of science and the result of its work will arise for the investigators and will require resolution.

Collectively, scientists cannot reconcile themselves with the religious or philosophical solution to the contradiction. They will seek a scientific solution.

VI.

Science is a singular unity and all domains of its expertise are, without exception, tightly connected. This empirical generalization is so rigorous that it cannot be changed by individual will.

There is more. We can say, in borrowing the comparison from another domain of human life, that science is profoundly democratic. All the work performed in the realm of science is fundamentally equivalent, for *sub specie aeternitatis [from the perspective of the eternal]* science contains nothing of importance, nor of unimportance, its efforts all lead to the same, unique scientific character, to the unique—and obligatory for all without exception—scientific comprehension of the surrounding environment.

This conviction guides, in the most profound and inevitable fashion, all scientific workers.

But the belief in the scientific work produced by the majority of scientific investigators, that the phenomena having to do with the study of life will finally arrive at penetrating into the scientific picture of the universe, without producing fundamental changes in it—this faith irrevocably evokes, in the opinions of the scientist, a value quite different in different domains of scientific knowledge.

---

9. Italics added for emphasis here to clarify meaning.

This results in an acute instability in the scientific organization of humanity.

The primary admission that, by their essence, the mathematical, astronomical and physical-chemical sciences alone exercise an action on the comprehension of the fundamental bases of the present scientific picture of the universe—space, time, matter, energy—this admission which has often been expressed, but which has never really penetrated into the scientific environment, cannot be durable.

It cannot be, as a result of the ever-growing number of workers occupied by the study of living phenomena, owing to the results of their scientific work acquiring an increasingly strong influence on scientific thought, and their work exceeding the value, for scientific thought, of constructions of the scientific picture of the Cosmos. The history of the evolutionary ideas of the preceding century, which I have already pointed out, is instructive from this point of view.

Doubts are raised among naturalists, preventing them from admitting the primacy of the mathematical, astronomical, and physical-chemical sciences, a primacy inspired by the modern edifice of the scientific universe.

Two conclusions must inevitably give rise to the doubts of the empirical naturalist:

Cannot the life sciences effectively change the fundamental representations of the scientific universe—the representations of space, time, energy, matter—in a radical way? And is this list of fundamental elements of our scientific thought complete?

Can the naturalist seriously admit that the intelligence of *Homo sapiens faber* is the final manifestation of the evolution of species, the maximum of spiritual acquisition of organized beings? Or indeed, must it be believed that only the transitory spiritual possibilities of life are manifesting themselves before us on the Earth in the present geological epoch, and that there exist higher manifestations in this domain in some point of the Cosmos?

Without a negative response from science to these questions which inevitably arise, faith in the reality of the contemporary picture of the universe can include only a relatively limited number of scientific workers.

What's more, scientists do not inhabit an isolated island. Great creative work of humanity takes place all around them—fertile in many respects—in other spiritual domains, in religion and above all in philosophy, work which is absolutely contrary to the scientific conception created in the last centuries.

All this widens the contradiction which exists between scientific work and its fundamental, official result.

At present, the scientific organization of humanity lacks necessary stability and the result of scientific work is increasingly dissociated from its *content*[10] in the consciousness of scientists, whose numbers always increase.

VII.

Once such an instability in the essential instrument of scientific knowledge is recognized, this cannot continue.

This state of affairs has begun to change suddenly in the past decade following a new first-order event—the radical change of the physical sciences, in part, astronomical.

Space, time, matter and energy are clearly distinguished for the naturalist of the year 1929, from the space, time, matter and energy of the naturalist of 1900.

They are not only different; it is obvious that they cannot serve the scientific construction of the Cosmos, even under the clearly changed form under which they are currently manifest. New ideas are penetrating physics which draw the required attention of physicists to the phenomena of life. As it happens, these new ideas are expressed with greater clarity in the phenomena of life than in the ordinary objects of physical investigation. These traits, these elements of the construction neglected in the scientific picture of the universe, which change its Newtonian form, clearly cannot be grasped or studied until we introduce in some form the sciences of life into the picture of the Universe.

It is at the same time curious that the traits of life which had drawn little attention from biologists, today serve as the first-order phenomena of life.

It seems to me that the profound and growing change which is happening in the sciences of life under the influence of the crisis in physics is becoming clear in that way.

Before moving on to the problem of fundamental conceptions of life, now demanding attention and precision in connection with this crisis taking place in the

_____

10. Emphasis added for clarity.

Alexander I. Oparin (1894–1980), a contemporary of Vernadsky, was more of a political tool and opportunist than a serious scientist. Oparin, pictured here on the right during a visit in 1969 to NASA Ames Research Center, made it his life's work to argue the opposite point to that which Vernadsky sets forth in this paper, insisting that the origin of life, and even that of human cognition, could ultimately be explained by purely random reactions among non-living chemical building blocks. Oparin's fallacies continue to corrupt science today (See article: Rouillard, Meghan, "A.I. Oparin: Fraud, Fallacy, or Both," 21st Century Science & Technology, Spring 2013, p. 42).

historic progress of the physical sciences, I will say a few words about the characteristic traits of this crisis.

VIII.

As I clearly cannot dwell upon the changes taking place before our eyes in the fundamental notions of physics in any detail, I will only concern myself with some problems in the historical process which is unfolding, problems which will be necessary for me in the later report.

What is essential is the complete change in our notions of space, time, energy, gravitation, and matter. The force of universal gravitation, acting instantaneously upon every considerable distance, has disap-

peared without a trace from our thoughts. Space and time are inseparable, and to understand physical phenomena we are forced to geometrically employ space of not three, but of four dimensions. The boundary separating energy from matter fades. Energy is propagated in strictly determined jumps—quanta.

The reversal of opinions and representations was produced with great celerity, and was quite unstable. The physicists still thought, at the beginning of this century, much differently than we do today. I remember a conversation I had more than 20 years ago with P.N. Lebedev, the eminent Russian physicist, who told me he was only secure speaking about the ether. This was at the time when the notion of the electron began to enter into physics. Currently, physicists try not to speak of the ether and there are some who doubt its very existence.

At this time, at the beginning of the century, the dawn of dynamic representations of matter and of energy seemed to blossom along with the ether. Certain scientists of great scholarship, possessing a philosophical erudition, such as, for example, W. Ostwald senior, considered the atomistic representation of matter to have been definitively buried. There was an attempt to rid chemistry of it (Wald).[11] It happens that the contemporaries had not understood the process of scientific thought which was developed with their participation.

In two or three years, the atomic representation achieved an unprecedented success, and became dominant.

From then, it was only one or two years before we often heard affirmation that as of now the existence of the atom had really been proven and that the atomic theory of matter was no longer a theory, but a natural phenomenon which could be detected. The atomic theory of Bohr and Rutherford seemed to reign definitively. However, this reign came to an end. Today, the atom begins to fade from our minds, we speak of the wave theory of matter, on the one hand, and on the other, the impossibility of reducing phenomena to the motion of points in the areas of physics which treat the physics of the atom, of even smaller particles. The more

11. Vernadsky is likely referring to chemist František Wald (1861–1930). http://w ww.hyle.org/journal/issues/13-1/bio_ruthenberg.pdf

The revolutionary scientific discoveries of Albert Einstein (1879–1955) and Max Planck (1858–1947) represented the first major steps in the 20th century to overthrowing the old physics, and emphatically the ideas of Newton in the case of Einstein. Here, Planck and Einstein are pictured in Berlin with the German physicist Walther Nernst in 1931.

exact the determination of speed of motion of particle becomes, the less exact will be the determination of its geometric position. Mechanical laws of the motion of points cannot be applied to these phenomena with sufficient precision.

The old dynamic representations are reborn under a new form, as foreign to the old as atomic physics of the 20th century is to that of Gassendi.[12]

The change which opinions have undergone is very abrupt: there is no longer any established stability there, we will probably live for a long time in the fermentation of ideas which characterize the current state of physics. It is precisely this fermentation which will have influence upon the neighboring sciences. There had not been room there for irreversible processes in physico-chemical phenomena embraced by scientific theory in the picture of the Newtonian universe, which had reigned, at the beginning of this century. All natural processes in that context were always considered de facto as reversible. This principle constitutes the basis of the scientific

representation of a Cosmos of the 19th Century. In the case where they seemed to be irreversible, only an apparent irreversibility was assumed and the idea of a very slow development —to the point of being absurd—of a reversible process was accepted, which usually allowed for the management of any difficulties created by experiment and observation relatively well. Today, the irreversible process plays another role in physics—probably a very important role. This admission is of great significance for the problems which occupy us. All the conclusions have not yet been drawn. It is possible that the irreversible processes are dominant in the Universe, as they seem to constitute the essence of phenomena in molecular physics, in the physics of microscopic phenomena, in the phenomena of heat and radiant energy, and of light.

No less important is the distinction between statistical laws and laws treating the elements of physical processes themselves. I already mentioned the atoms which correspond to them and the characteristics of the application of the laws of motion of points to these.

It is a phenomenon common to all processes located in the internal structure of the Universe—molecular or microscopic according to the modern expression—for regions where the hypothetical universal gravitation has never been able to penetrate.

Here is a case where the law of causality, in the regular sense, seems to cease to be applicable or is no longer present. This law of causality is the alpha and omega of the picture of the Newtonian universe. The idea on which it is based is clearly expressed by Laplace in his acceptance of the possibility of encompassing the Universe in a unique formula whose solution allows for the calculation of the motions of the planets, the development of thought, the motion of reeds, and the change of state of spiral nebulae.[13] Such determin-

---

12. A reference to Pierre Gassendi (1592–1655), a French scientist and astronomer known as an early proponent of the atom theory of matter.

13. Known as "LaPlace's Demon." From the horse's mouth: "An intellect which at a certain moment would know all forces that set nature in motion, and all positions of all items of which nature is composed, if this intellect were also vast enough to submit these data to analysis, it would embrace in a single formula the movements of the greatest bodies of the universe and those of the tiniest atom; for such an intellect nothing would be uncertain and the future just like the past would be present before its eyes." Pierre-Simon Laplace,

ism disappeared for a determined category of physical phenomena in modern physics. It is not insignificant that for these cases some physicists saw that there was not only an analogy with the biological individual, but a phenomenon of the same logical category. In the best case the unpredictable coefficients, from a quantitative point of view, will become part of the classical formula of Laplace.

There is nothing great or small in nature. If we admit such a disparity in the action of causality—for example of the impossibility of expressing everything by the laws of motion—we will inevitably be forced to come to the same admission in other cases.

The analogies between the infinitely small of the molecular world and the grandiose bodies and spaces of the stellar world are numerous and real. It is always necessary to have this correction in view. The new physics today begins to accept, by the intermediary of its numerous representatives, the principle destroying at its very root the representation of the infinity of the Cosmos, which Bruno had caused to penetrate into the understanding of the Universe of modern times. The idea of the possible boundary of the Cosmos, the finiteness of its space, is beginning to enter into scientific representations under a new guise. Certainly the dimensions of this Cosmos are very vast. Its volume is no less than a radius equivalent to 10^{17}–10^{18} km, that is, say quintillions of kilometers, and the importance does not lie in the dimensions, but rather in the fact that the volume of the world has limits, that it is bounded. That is where its immense importance lies. In this way, we are actually approaching the Middle Ages of Dante with his bounded universe, more than the infinite space of the scientists of the 16th–19th Centuries.[14]

The change goes even further. We are clearly approaching the distinction between the space of physics and the space of geometry. The principle of symmetry is beginning to penetrate physics. We cannot, for example, understand in any other way the problem recently posed for purposes of experimental investigation regarding the speed of the propagation of light: is it identical in the two directions along the same line?[15]

Pierre-Simon Laplace (1749–1827), whose theory of deterministic causality Vernadsky ridicules as accepting "the possibility of encompassing the Universe in a single formula whose solution allows for the calculation of the motions of the planets, the development of thought, the motion of reeds, and the change of state of spiral nebulae" (Posthumous portrait by Jean-Baptiste Paulin Guêrin).

Certainly all the new acquisitions and this boldness will not remain stable in science; they imply that the old Newtonian representation of the Universe had created a crack, its scientific certitude shaken and an infinite and ever-growing throng of new representations made due to this crack have created an opening allowing for a sudden burst all the more rapidly.

The scientific representation of the Universe based on universal gravitation and on the physico-chemical phenomena of which we have spoken and which people have thought about for three centuries—must break down.

The scientific picture of the Universe based on universal gravitation and on the possibility of scientifically expressing all ambient motion of particles by reversible processes, by a rigorous determinism calculated in advance, this picture changes and does not correspond to facts. The individual begins to penetrate into the world of physical phenomena.

Essai philosophique sur les probabilités (1814)

14. This concept seems to be most clearly represented in Dante Alighieri's *Divina Commedia*, which poetically describes nine celestial spheres of heaven. This is depicted in the captioned image.

15. This could be a reference to Michelson-Morley type experiments which continued into the 1920's and even later to test for this kind of phenomenon.

The elements of the Cosmos which constitute its existence, considered at the level of a microscopic cross-section, have, it is possible, profound analogies with living individuals and organisms.

The order of Nature is other than had been believed. To reduce the entire environment to what had been conceived, was found, in the final analysis, to be too simplified and approximate.

IX.

This radical change of fundamental physical representations must inevitably have a clear impact on the position of living phenomena in the edifice of the scientific Universe, as a great number of admissions of the new physics are in no way expressed with as much clarity as in life phenomena: such as, for example, the irreversible character, in time, of physico-chemical processes observed in living organisms. The irreversible cycle in the time of the phenomena characterize life to a degree unknown in the crude nature which surrounds us. The irreversibility characterizes the life of the individual, and is clearly expressed for us in its death. The irreversibility is no less clearly expressed in the process of the evolution of species in the course of geological time.

The irreversible process of evolution, its direction determined in the same unique sense can be followed from the Algonquin Era[16] until today.

It was certainly known for a long time, but not much importance was attributed to it, although its contradiction with the assertion of the possibility of reducing the phenomena of life to physico-chemical processes accepted in the Newtonian universe was understood. It is a very common manifestation of a lack of breadth of our logical analysis in the domain of scientific thought; perhaps inevitable given the complexity of the Cosmos and the weakness of the scientific instrument which serves us in penetrating into the unknown.

The phenomena of life, of radioactivity, of the interior of stars, are probably the most clear manifestations of irreversible processes in surrounding nature. This type of process finds its most distinct expression in the phenomena of life.

But this expression in living processes, which is so clear, of a physical phenomenon of nature which is absolutely cosmic, is not accidental or unique. The same

observed fact is seen in the properties of space and it can also be indicated in energetic processes, in the properties of matter which construct living matter.

These consequences of life for the fundamental notions of the Order of the Universe compel us to introduce the phenomena of life into the universe of the new physics.

In the presence of the unity of all that lives, of life, we cannot know where the penetration of the scientifically constructed Cosmos by the phenomena of life will stop. In this respect, the future is probably full of big surprises.

It is necessary to approach this process, whose progress seems inevitable to me, in another way, in relying upon the scientific conceptions of life.

It is important to pay attention to the phenomena of life whose introduction in the domain of the scientific construction of the Universe is already beginning to become probable.

We are approaching a very rational epoch—and that of a radical change in our conception of the scientific Universe.

This change will not be, in its consequences, any less important than it was at the time of the creation of the Cosmos, based upon universal gravitation, and infinite time and space, the Cosmos penetrated by matter and energy.

This change will allow us to overcome the contradiction which exists between life and scientific creation on the one hand, and the scientifically constructed Cosmos on the other, a contradiction which is clearly apparent during the 16th–19th Centuries, the time of the creation and the development of the Newtonian Universe. This was, incidentally, the conception of the Universe of Newton without Newton, who had introduced to it the corrections of a believing Christian.[17]

The possibility of overcoming the contradiction while dwelling only within the boundaries of science, appears to be opening up to us today.

---

16. More commonly known today as the Pre-Cambrian Era.

17. While hard to definitively interpret this sentence, one can rightfully detect some sarcasm in Vernadsky's reference to Newton as a believing Christian. It should be noted that in the person of Newton, we find a mixture of both dead reductionism and wild "religious" speculation: Newton was known to have posited the idea that God should be able to intervene and wind up the Universe at his will to prevent it from running down, a point he debated through his intermediary Samuel Clarke with Wilhelm Gottfried Leibniz. *"God Almighty wants to wind up his watch from time to time: otherwise it would cease to move. He had not, it seems, sufficient foresight to make it a perpetual motion."* Quote is taken from The Leibniz-Clarke correspondence.

X.

There is no doubt that life in the scientific picture of the Universe will appear to us in an unexpected form. All phenomena studied in physics and chemistry manifest themselves there in another form than that which they present to our sense organs.

Let us dwell on several phenomena of life, which at this moment require attention, due to changes taking place in physics.

I am not a biologist and I consider phenomena of life from another point of view than that which is customary in biology—their action on the cosmic environment of their life. Claude Bernard, one of the greatest biologists of the past century, always employed this expression—cosmic environment—when speaking of life. He clearly understood that life is not an insignificant terrestrial phenomenon, but a cosmic manifestation.

Many manifestations of life in this domain, quite worthy of attention, can be noted, some of which take on a planetary character, connected with the Earth, whereas others clearly exceed the limits of planetary existence, indicating the more general situation of life in the Cosmos.

Among the notable planetary properties of of life are:

1) Living matter is created and maintained on our planet by the cosmic energy of the Sun. There, it forms an integral part of the upper geosphere, the biosphere, an indissoluble part of its mechanism.
2) Solar energy is gradually transported by the intermediary of living matter into the deepest parts of the planet, its crust.
3) The quantity of matter in the biosphere penetrated by life is a constant value or almost permanent across geological time.[18]

A fresco by Domenico di Michelino (1465) showing Dante Alighieri (1265–1321) holding a copy of his Divine Comedy, *with its seven terraces of purgatory and nine spheres of heaven depicted in the background. Vernadsky refers to Dante's work as an early example of an idea of a bounded universe.*

4) Living matter enters, in the course of all geological time and in a uniform way, into the geochemical cycles of the chemical elements in the Earth's crust, playing a very important role there. In this way, living matter provides a determined geochemical energy in the migration of terrestrial chemical elements, energy whose primary is the Sun.
5) Living matter is in a continual chemical exchange with the cosmic environment that surrounds it, but is never spontaneously generated there. In the course of all geological time, this living matter represents a unique unity, genetically linked, and clearly separated from this cosmic environment.
6) Biogenic geochemical energy tends toward its maximum manifestation in the biosphere (first biogeochemical principle).
7) In the course of the evolution of species, it is the organisms which augment, through their life, biogenic geochemical energy, which survive (the second bio-

---

18. Vernadsky seems to change his view later, in 1938. In "Problems of Biogeochemistry II" he states: *"The mass of living matter of the biosphere is close to the limit and, evidently, remains a relatively constant value on the scale of historical time. It is determined, above all, by the radiant energy of the Sun, falling on the biosphere, and by the biogeochemical energy of the process of colonization of the planet. Evidently, the mass of living matter increases in the course of geological time, and the process of the occupation of the Earth's crust by living matter has not yet been completed."*

Francesco Redi (1626–1697), an Italian poet, naturalist, and physician who was first to enunciate the principle of "omne vivum ex vivo," or "all life comes from life," thus challenging the belief in spontaneous generation. This concept is referred to by Vernadsky as Redi's Principle.

geochemical principle).

8) In the course of the evolution of species, the chemical composition of living matter remains constant, but the biogenic geochemical energy provided by living matter in the cosmic environment increases.

9) With the appearance of man in the biosphere, conforming to the second biogeochemical principle, the action of life on our planet develops and changes by the effect of his intelligence to such an extent, that it becomes possible to speak of a special psychozoic epoch in the history of our planet, analogous to other geological epochs in the change effected in living nature on Earth, as during the Cambrian or Oligocene, for example. With the appearance of a living being on our planet gifted with intelligence, we pass into another stage of its history.

What is even more, here we clearly go beyond the limits of the planet, as everything indicates that the progress of the geochemical action of intelligence, of the life of civilized humanity, goes beyond the limits of the planet.

We see here a manifestation of life which, al-though being located on our planet, indicates properties of living things seemingly not bound by it. Let us note several of the most profound manifestations of life:

1) Human intelligence and the activity of life, organized by this intelligence, change the progress of natural processes and similarly they change the other manifestations of energy known to us, but in a new way.

2) This activity is regulated by the second biogeochemical principle, that is, that it tends towards the maximum manifestation [of biogeochemical energy].

3) We have never observed on Earth the formation of a living organism from abiotic matter without the participation of another organism (Redi's principle—irreversible process).

4) Organisms constitute autonomous systems which, in the cosmic environment, create volumes (thermodynamic fields) whose temperature and pressure are particular to them, distinguishing them from their environment.

5) Organisms can live in the environment of molecular forces, foreign to the laws of gravitation, as well as in the environment which these laws characterize. Their minimum dimensions reach 10^{-6} cm.; they penetrate into the domain of molecules.

6) The smaller the organism, the more intense its geochemical energy, the more quickly it creates new organisms. The maximum speed of this creation (division) has determined limits. I will call it the *element of biological time*. Today, I will again return to this phenomenon.

7) The life of the organism is an irreversible process which ends sooner or later with death. All living matter which penetrates the biosphere is overall an irreversible process in geological time; in the succession of generations we observe neither the beginning nor the end of this process and it could be that they do not exist.

8) It is not a diminution of free energy, but a growth which is effected in the cosmic environment resulting from life. In this case, life proceeds in a manner contrary to the law of entropy. Very few other physical phenomena in the Cosmos are on par with life according to this point of view: as, for example, radioactive bodies. But the cause of this phenomenon in living matter is clearly different.

9) The thermodynamic field of the living organism possesses, contrary to the properties of the cosmic envi-

ronment, a clearly expressed dissymmetry. We know of nothing similar for other natural bodies on Earth. The dissymmetry is expressed there as with the particular character of the symmetry of space, occupied by living matter, the existence of very clearly expressed polar, enantiomorphic vectors, but above all, the pronounced lack of conformity which distinguishes the right-handed from that of the left-handed character of phenomena (Generalization of Pasteur).

10) The activity of organisms, at least that of its most developed forms, is not a purely mechanical process which could be calculated. This activity is individual and diverse for different individuals. The degree of its freedom of action is not clear, but it is different in each case and can always be established.

XI.

This list is not complete, but it indicates, with evidence, that life manifests itself in the Cosmos in other forms than those which biology normally displays.

What is important, from the point of view of the scientific picture of the Universe, is that the investigation of life indicates such traits of the structure of the Cosmos, which in other phenomena studied by science are completely lacking or are very weakly or indistinctly expressed. In that way only the study of life changes the scientific picture of the Cosmos, formed without its contribution, and reveals new traits about it. It changes, essentially, the representation of space, time, energy, and other fundamental elements of the structure of the world.

Here I will dwell upon two phenomena which will allow for the clarification of the important role which the investigation of life plays in the scientific picture of the Universe, created by the new physics: in particular the phenomenon of the dissymmetry of the space of living organisms and the phenomenon of biological time.

In the first case, this is a matter of new properties (a particular state of physical space), observed in living organisms, and in the second, new properties of physical time.

Louis Pasteur (1822–1895), whose unique discoveries concerning the characteristic dissymmetries of living matter informed much of Vernadsky's work, along with the discoveries of Pierre Curie. Vernadsky states: "The weeds of oblivion have covered the path trodden by Pasteur and Curie. It seems to me that it is precisely by that path that the current wave of scientific work must now continue forward."

The dissymmetry of living matter was discovered 80 years ago—in 1848—by one of the greatest scientists of the past century, Louis Pasteur, who clarified its importance for the structure of the scientific Universe. Pasteur conceived of dissymmetry as a cosmic phenomenon and drew from it very important conclusions for the knowledge of life. His works must today draw the most diligent attention of the new physics. He returned several times to these ideas, always going deeper. He returned to them for the last time in a more developed form, in 1883, 46 years ago, and regretted not being able to get deeper into it experimentally; he considered this discovery as the most important work of his entire life, as the most profound penetration of his genius into the problems of science.

The fate of his ideas was peculiar: the main idea which Pasteur emphasized has not, up until today, penetrated scientific thought. The public opinion of chemists considered its basis as doubtful.

It seems to me that this depends upon the fact that

Pierre Curie (1858–1906), who continued the work of Pasteur in the study of symmetry, which he considered to be a "state of space" according to Vernadsky. As Vernadsky understood it, "Curie's Principle," that "all dissymmetry comes from dissymmetry," offers a new perspective on Redi's Principle, "all life comes from life." Portrait by Dujardin, c.1906.

chemists never took into account, in all its breadth, the notion of dissymmetry, on which Pasteur relied, and that this notion had not been understood by his contemporaries.

It was submitted to a serious analysis by another brilliant Frenchman, Pierre Curie, in 1894. The formulation of ideas of P. Curie is exceptionally concise, which could make them appear abstract, but his main theorem—on dissymmetry—allows for no doubt and is clear in its concrete importance for the naturalist. It states:

"The elements of symmetry of causes must be found in the effects, and the elements of dissymmetry of effects must be found in the causes."

The principle of Curie irrevocably resolves the dispute in favor of Pasteur, regarding his statements which call for research into the cause of the dissymmetry of natural bodies in life phenomena.

The fate of the works of Curie, were, in this area, analogous to that of Pasteur. Prevented from continuing this work due to the discovery of radioactivity, he returned, before his death in 1906, 23 years ago, to works on symmetry; judging from his journal notes, he had arrived at great generalizations in this domain. After his death—he was crushed by a cart in the streets of Paris—nobody picked up the thread he left, which slipped away from later physical analysis: the principle of symmetry, an analysis which concerns us in particular today.

The weeds of oblivion have covered the path tread by Pasteur and Curie. It seems to me that it is precisely by that path that the current wave of scientific work must now continue forward.

It has been six years since the eminent Dutch chemist F. Jaeger, who profoundly penetrated the phenomena of symmetry, called upon chemists to return to these ideas of Pasteur. His call was only met with a weak response. However, since then, the development of science has demanded the following of this path, to return to Pasteur and to P. Curie, who deepened Pasteur's ideas.

XII.

The phenomena of symmetry have not up until now been sufficiently embraced by philosophical and scientific thought. It is without any doubt the most fundamental and profound notion, which penetrates, in a subconscious way, our entire concept of the universe.

The revolution occurring in physics and the inevitable development of biological ideas tied to it, pose what seems to me to be the order of the day, the necessity of deepening and clarifying the principle of symmetry.

The most serious attempt of the study of symmetry, but which was not not completely followed through, was carried out by P. Curie, who considered symmetry fundamentally as a *state of space*, that is to say, as a structure of physical space.

This determination must be taken into consideration at the present time for the analysis of physical time, as in natural processes "space" and "time" are inseparable.

We can pursue the philosophical and mathematical

analysis of the doctrine of symmetry more profoundly, but for our problem, and remaining within the empirical universe of the naturalist, this conception of symmetry, broad and real, is sufficient.

The phenomena of symmetry have, overall, drawn the attention of physicists only in the 20th century when the enormous importance of crystallography with all its branches was definitively clarified in the domain of the physical sciences.

It is by way of crystallography and mineralogy that the doctrine of symmetry entered into physics. Even the most mathematical parts of this doctrine were elaborated with great precision and depth by mineralogists, who in this case always considered first their own problems, the problems of crystallography. Their acquisitions had been insufficient for physics, just as was proved by Pierre Curie.

They are insufficient in their current form, for the phenomena of life, which historically gave birth to the notion of symmetry itself, as this notion had its origin at the time of the work of sculptors who modeled living objects. The ancient Hellenes attributed the first formulation of the notion of symmetry in connection with the problem of the reproduction of the human body to Pythagoras of Rhegium, who lived more than 2,400 years ago.

And later, one of the founders of the doctrine of symmetry in mineralogy, A. Bravais, the eccentric French scientist, took symmetry, manifested in plants, as a point of departure for his work and created the doctrine of symmetry, basing his work simultaneously upon plants, minerals, and geometrical polyhedra.

But whereas the study of natural crystals blossomed in light of the doctrine of symmetry, the application of symmetry to living objects to which it owes its origin, and to physical phenomena, has always been sporadic and detached.

This had repercussions for the position of the doctrine of symmetry in contemporary scientific organization. The doctrine of symmetry is ordinarily connected to the teaching of mineralogy and the neighboring sciences, and does not hold the place which is due it, either in the discipline of physics, or of biology.

This is apparent in the lack of precision of representations of symmetry, which do not matter much for either crystallography or mineralogy, and in particular in the notion of dissymmetry, the importance of which was noted by L. Pasteur (for biology) and by P. Curie (for physics).

XIII.

The term dissymmetry refers to diverse phenomena. For living bodies, for example, we can indicate two such phenomena which are demonstrated there simultaneously, but which are nonetheless independent. One of these phenomena is related to the doctrine of symmetry, whereas the other is not at all, but can only be studied on the basis of it.

In elaborating his great empirical generalization, Pasteur noted simultaneously the two phenomena in the state of space of living organisms.

At his time, even the notion of symmetry itself did not correspond to the current doctrine.

Although J. Hessel[19] had resolved, fifteen years before Pasteur, the problem of symmetry in a general form for crystals, his work did not draw much attention and did not enter life[20] for another thirty years, well after the discoveries of Pasteur. Pasteur had not yet reunited holohedry with hemihedry as we do today.[21] He did not realize that the optical and crystalline properties are always different manifestations of the same phenomenon—the phenomenon of symmetry—just as we now accept it.[22] He found this connection in a particular case, and upon this basis, constructed his terminology, which did not enter later into common usage and which is rarely used even in his own country, in France. We find the same terminology in a more general form, in a more precise construction of Curie, which he does not indicate.

In studying the crystalline forms of organic compounds, existing in organisms or derived from them, Pasteur noticed the diminution of their symmetry, the appearance of forms—left and right,—in the case where the racemic bodies were split up into their left and right antipodes. He called this phenomenon dis-

19. Johann Friedrich Christian Hessel MD, PhD (1796–1872), a German physician and professor of mineralogy who made significant contributions to the field of crystallography.

20. The meaning of the word life (*vie*) is unclear here, as far as whether it refers to ideas affecting the study of life per se, or the life of scientists more generally.

21. Holohedry and hemihedry relate to the symmetry of faces. In hemihedry there is, speaking generally, less symmetry, as for example, in the irregular shapes which are found on tartaric acid crystals, which Louis Pasteur studied. The faces of the tartaric acid crystals are said to be hemihedral.

22. Right-handed tartaric acid is said to rotate light and be "hemihedral" in the same direction; its corners being truncated. See picture of two tartaric acid crystals.

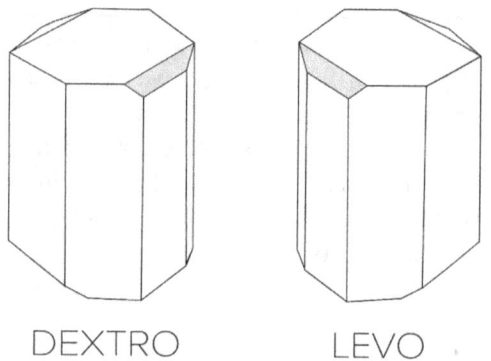

DEXTRO   LEVO

Examples of dextrotartaric and levotartaric acid crystals. Note that the truncated corners of the two different tartaric acid crystals (shaded) are what show their chiral character. Tartaric acid is a by-product of fermentation and can be found in the residues of wine.

symmetry, that is, the violation of symmetry, as with regard to the polyhedra of racemic compounds the violation of symmetry was expressed by the regular lack of either right or left faces of the antipodes.

He noticed that the polyhedra formed in this way were lacking centers and planes of symmetry whereas the fundamental polyhedra of racemic compounds, by the separation of which compounds the right and left antipodes had been obtained, possessed a center and planes of symmetry.[23]

He simultaneously proved that whereas the racemic polyhedra were optically inert in solution, the solutions of their antipodes rotated the planes of polarization—the right ones to the right, the left ones to the left.

He considered these two phenomena as a demonstration of the phenomenon of dissymmetry and as this demonstration remains stable in the liquid state, he named it *molecular dissymmetry*, seeking an explanation of the phenomenon in the structure of the chemical molecules.

Here, I cannot present the current composition of the phenomenon discovered by Pasteur. But it is important, however, to dwell upon it a bit.

Today we know that among the 32 classes of crystals, 13 correspond to the dissymmetry of Pasteur, that is to say that they don't possess any centers or planes of symmetry, but, with the exception of one single case, have axes of symmetry, which turn the planes of polar-

ization to the right or left in determined vectors and which give right polyhedra in the first case and left in the second.

In addition, we know that these properties of crystals are expressed by the helicoidal distribution of their atoms—right and left—as required by the molecular dissymmetry of Pasteur.

But this dissymmetry is only manifested in solutions, in liquids in the case where we observe, in the chemical structure, materials known to Pasteur, the so-called asymmetric carbon to which all the bonds are united to diverse atoms or groups of atoms. In the formulas of the chemists, the asymmetric carbon can actually lack even one element of symmetry in the surrounding space; it can be truly asymmetric. But the entire space of the molecule in which it is located will be dissymmetric, that is, it will possess some[24] axes of symmetry.

We are still awaiting more developments in the domain of the phenomena of symmetry. But at the same time, Pasteur discovered a new phenomenon while studying the phenomena of dissymmetry in relation to living matter, also related to the diminution of symmetry, that is to say the dissymmetry which, however, is located outside of the domain of the phenomena of symmetry and cannot be explained or predicted by it.

He discovered that in certain cases, instead of two antipodes, right and left, appearing simultaneously and in equal number, as required by the laws of symmetry, only one of the two antipodes emerges, or one of the two predominates clearly over the other.

As Pasteur did not, in general, know that one part of the violation of symmetry—which he called dissymmetry—could, actually, be deduced from the laws of symmetry, he did not distinguish this type of dissymmetry from other types which he had discovered, treating them as phenomena of the same type; however, he noticed that the latter phenomenon was exclusively connected with life, whereas the former could be independent of it.

From the physical point of view, these two phenomena, both called dissymmetrical, are fundamentally distinct. The first is related to the distribution of objects in

---

23. Referring to the just cited image of tartaric acid crystals can help with envisioning this.

24. Word "some" added here for clarity. The distinction is that something asymmetric will have no axes of symmetry, whereas something dissymmetric will have some axes of symmetry, as well as axes of dissymmetry.

space, studied by the doctrine of symmetry. The second is not related to symmetry and is a real violation of it which cannot be predicted on the basis of symmetry.[25]

The principle of Curie, according to which every phenomena possessing dissymmetry must result from a cause, possessing the same dissymmetry, is so general that it includes both phenomena.

XIV.

Before expounding on the acquisitions of Pasteur, let us dwell upon the character of space which stems from symmetry, on its distinction from that of our space, the space of physics and geometry. It is precisely this specific space which we observe everywhere in organisms, conforming to the discovery of Pasteur and the principle of Curie—in the interior of bacteria or of the elephant for example. Certain properties of such a—let us call it—enantiomorphic space—right or left—must be apparent outside, in the surrounding environment of organisms during their life.

The distinction of such a space from regular space can be clearly expressed by the study of physical properties of vectors which are found there: that is, by the study of direction.

I already indicated that the phenomena of life are irreversible in time, that it to say, they always advance with the progress of time in one direction, without retracing their steps. The organism grows, ages, and ends in death.

There are no reversible phenomena: man has only imagined them in fairy tales and fantasies. In certain cases the signs of a reversible process can be observed [as the eminent Russian zoologist Schmidt[26] and recently C. Davidoff showed]. But it is not these particular phenomena which characterize the life of the individual and the evolution of species.

Geometrically, the time of such a process can be be expressed in the form of a vector AB, which is not identical to BA (–). The time of such a process is at least lacking a center of symmetry (the physicists sometimes incorrectly call it asymmetrical time). Whereas for the

LEFT-HANDED   RIGHT-HANDED

QUARTZ

Above, a representation of the molecules of amino acids, and below, quartz crystals. Solutions of organic matter, from life, can rotate a plane of polarized light, but dissolved quartz, which is inorganic, does not. They are both dissymmetric, but not in the same way.

reversible process, AB=BA. The two vectors there are identical.

We can express this phenomenon by calling the first vectors *polar*, and the second *isotropic*. Time is geometrically expressed in the phenomena of life by polar vectors, and in regular phenomena—by isotropic vectors.

Space and time are inseparable in the new physics as well as in the real world of the naturalist. The ideas of Einstein are closer in this sense to the scientific concepts of the naturalist than the ideas of Newton, where time does not appear in the force of gravitation.

This explains the difficulty that the Newtonian

---

25. It appears that Vernadsky is talking about the structure of the crystals as the first case, and secondly the optical rotation in solution. Handed crystals, such as quartz, exist, but do not exhibit the rotation of polarized light that solutions made from organic compounds do.

26. Likely a reference to Peter (Petr) Schmidt, who appears to have been a zoologist and professor in St. Petersburg, in addition to possibly holding more posts.

theory has seen in penetrating the scientific environment, having required 2–3 generations to be accepted, and the celerity with which it has disappeared today from our field of view.[27][28]

The characteristic polar vectors for time therefore also have to characterize space, that is to say, the volume occupied by the bodies of organisms.

The phenomena of dissymmetry, characteristic, according to Pasteur, of these bodies, not only confirm this fact, but indicate again that these polar vectors must be *enantiomorphic*.

The direction AB is distinct from that of BA, but simultaneously, motion in the right and left directions around the vector in its surrounding environment can be as physically distinct. We distinguish the right and left vectors according to the helical direction of objects or motions in relation to the given vector. We distinguish, in this way, between four vectors upon one line:

AB (+)........... right and left;
BA (–).......... right and left.

---

27. [The brilliant and interesting lessons of M. Eddington on the nature of the physical world (1929) allow us, for example, to judge the depth with which the concept of the Universe of Newton has penetrated today, in its scientific part—the independence of space from time—into scientific opinion. In setting out the fundamental ideas of the new physics M. Eddington based himself on the Universe of Einstein in which space and time are inseparable. And yet he admitted that the nature and the role of physical time, comparatively to that of physical space, was something else altogether. Recognizing, for the notion of time, a logical genesis of double nature—investigation of the external and internal experience of the living being (man)—he did not admit the same fact for space, not recognizing that these two phenomena were inseparable, according to the concept of the Universe of Einstein, and that these two were equally included in the particularities of the "space-time" of the living being. Incomprehensibly, he did not take into account the discovery of Pasteur, of the particular state of space of life.]

28. Based on a still in progress reading of the referenced book, "The Nature of the Physical World" (1929), Eddington is at least in part referring to the debate initiated by Henri Bergson, whom Eddington refers to, regarding a concept of time which he called "la durée" or the psychological experience of time, which Bergson says is not touched by the theory of relativity. In the cited book, Eddington chooses to make the explicit point that there is no such psychological notion of space: "When I close my eyes and retreat into my inner mind, I feel myself enduring, I do not feel myself extensive. It is this feeling of time as affecting ourselves and not merely as existing in the relations of external events which is so peculiarly characteristic of it; space on the other hand is always appreciated as something external." It is not clear is Bergson made this point himself. Vernadsky referenced Bergson's concept of "durée" in "The Problem of Time in Contemporary Science." A book review by Vernadsky of Eddington's book exists in Russian. It appears that Vernadsky is taking issue with Eddington's statements implying that the main characteristic of space is simply extension.

In the case where certain single vectors—right or left—predominate in space, there we distinguish between two distinct spaces, right and left. This is what Pasteur discovered for the phenomena of life.

We can and must go further.

The doctrine of symmetry includes a fundamental principle, indicating that the real structure of space where that structure appears is characterized by the minimum symmetry of phenomena observed there. It follows that there cannot be a center of symmetry in cosmic space, studied by physics, because otherwise we would not have observed polar vectors in one of its phenomena, but this space also cannot be characterized by planes of symmetry, as there would not then be enantiomorphic vectors in its other phenomenon, in the domain of life.

The space as well as the time of the old physics was isotropic: the vectors there corresponded, in their properties, to ordinary lines.

The space of the new physics is anisotropic. It can only include, in extreme cases, axes of symmetry. It is possible that this space is completely asymmetric, that is, that it does not possess any axes of symmetry. In this case, its properties, the properties of everything, will not be predicted by the doctrine of symmetry: all vectors will be polar, enantiomorphic and different in their numerical size.

The study of the physico-chemical properties of the field of life gives us, from this point of view, the most precise and profound indications, unlike any other phenomenon, meanwhile, of the Cosmos of physics.

XV.

Now let us focus our attention on the state of space embraced by life, as it appears to us in light of the discoveries of Pasteur, which remain until now the basis of our knowledge in this domain.

There exist a large number of biological observations related to the same domain which confirm the generalization of Pasteur, but they are disperse, not systematized, and not coordinated by thought in general.

I will return to this again; now, I take up the discoveries of Pasteur.

Pasteur unquestionably settled the matter of the dissymmetric structure—the absence of a center of symmetry and planes of symmetry—for all the main compounds produced by organisms and their products. The

Vernadsky said that while mankind is, in one respect, a living creature, he is set absolutely apart from all lower forms of life. For example, he is not bound to planet Earth. Above, a photograph taken by astronaut Bill Anders of Apollo 8 of the "Earthrise" above the lunar horizon on December 24, 1968.

erals with a helicoidal distribution of atoms in space (for example, quartz crystals). But the number of antipodes among the inorganic bodies of nature is never unequal. In the same deposits, we encounter right and left-handed quartz crystals of equal number. The contrary fact is observed for the compounds of living things.

At first glance, Pasteur had considered that the phenomena of life were distinguished from inorganic phenomena by their molecular dissymmetry, by their connection with the distribution of molecules (and respectively their atoms) in space. This distinction has disappeared for us; the dissymmetry of quartz is also connected to the distribution of atoms of silicon and oxygen in space.

Later, and to this day, the character of dissymmetry, discovered by Pasteur, was explained by the specific asymmetry of the carbon atom in the molecules of compounds, introduced by Le Bel and Van 't Hoff. But we are currently discovering other asymmetric atoms in molecules, such as Al, N, etc.

The phenomenon is probably connected to the stability of classes of symmetry in the solid state, without centers or planes of symmetry, for molecules having asymmetric atomic fields. This is only observed in nature in living organisms.

Pasteur deduced from this, with good reason, that such a clear difference between the matter of living organisms and abiotic matter had to be closely connected to the fundamental properties of the manifestation of life, and that it inevitably required particular cosmic forces by whose action life becomes manifest. He said:

"If the immediate principles of life are dissymmetric, it is because, in their development, dissymmetric cosmic forces preside; it is there, according to me, that one of the connections between life on the surface of the Earth and the Cosmos, that is, the totality of forces spread throughout the universe, lies."[29]

And again:

experience of more than half a century of biochemistry absolutely confirms this fact.

He named this dissymmetry molecular, as it is not only manifested in crystals, but in the liquid phase and in solutions. It is related to the helicoidal distribution of atoms in space, conforming to the laws of the symmetry of crystals. Albumins, fats, carbohydrates, the alkaloids, hydrocarbons, and sugars are all dissymmetric. All chemical bodies making up grains and eggs are without exception clearly dissymmetric.

Natural inorganic compounds, inorganic minerals, in no case manifest such a dissymmetry, that is to say that the property of rotating the plane of polarization of light in the liquid state or in solutions, is not present in them.

The deduction of Pasteur showing that molecular dissymmetry characterized the matter of living organisms and that it was not observed in the cosmic environment of surrounding life, remains unshakeable.

In this environment, we only know of petroleums which possess molecular dissymmetry and certain min-

---

29. [Oeuvres (Works) of Pasteur, Tome (Volume) I, 373.] (Translator has located this quote on p. 375)

Adam Blick/Mount Lemmon Sky Center/U. of Arizona

ESO

Vernadsky, as did Louis Pasteur before him, hypothesized that there might be a real connection between the handedness of life on Earth, and manifestations of handedness in the cosmos, such as spiral galaxies, seen above in the cases of galaxies M51 and M74. Pasteur said, "I see dissymmetry everywhere in the universe."

"I see dissymmetry everywhere in the universe. Because we are coming to see that there had only been one single case where the right molecules differed from their left, the case where they are subjected to actions of a dissymmetric order. These dissymmetrical actions, possibly placed under cosmic influences, do these reside in light, electricity, magnetism, or heat? Would they be related to the motion of the Earth, with the electric currents by which physicists explain the terrestrial magnetic poles?"[30]

"What could be the nature of these dissymmetric actions? I think, for my part, that they are of a cosmic order. The universe is a dissymmetrical unity, and I am convinced that life, such as it presents itself to us, is a function of the dissymmetry of the universe or of the consequences to which it leads. The motion of light from the sun is dissymmetric."[31]

It is very characteristic that it is *one single antipode* which predominates or exists exclusively in the compounds connected with life. The other appears not at all,

or only rarely, although it is possible to obtain it in the laboratory. I will note that following the principle of Curie, our chemical synthesis is provoked by a dissymmetrical cause expressed by the intelligence and the will of the experimenter.

Pasteur considered that only the right-handed forms of matter were stable in living organisms, that is, that the space occupied by life favors only the preservation of these molecular structures. He thought that we only observed right-handed antipodes in the most important matter of organisms—in seeds and eggs.

In short, the generalization of Pasteur, which unfortunately did not draw sufficient attention from the biochemists, holds true, although the right or left character of compounds is a more complex phenomenon than Pasteur believed.

The principal fact is the stability of one antipode in the field of life and the disappearance of the other. The predominance of the right antipode finds no current explanation; incidentally, the stability of a single antipode and not of other also has no explanation.

Pasteur was always concerned with this problem. He said:

"To understand the exclusive formation of molecules of a single order of dissymmetry it there-

---

30. [Works, I, 361 (1860).] (Translator has located this quote on p. 341)
31. [Works, I, 341 (1860).] (Translator has located this quote on page 361)

fore suffices to admit that *at the moment of their grouping the elemental atoms are subjected to a dissymmetric influence* and as all other organic molecules which were given birth to in analogous circumstances are identical, whatever the origin and place of their production may be, *this influence should be universal.* It encompasses the entire terrestrial globe."[32]

This phenomenon puts a very clear limit between the enantiomorphic forms created in the thermodynamic field of life and those of the surrounding cosmic environment where they are also located.

It is important to note that in the unique group of minerals characterized by molecular symmetry—in petroleums—we observe, first of all, their genesis by the metamorphosis of the remains of living matter, and second, the marked predominance of right-handed rotation in petroleums. Left-handed petroleums are very rare.

Ten years after his generalization, Pasteur went further and established a new fact in this domain which is no less important. It was in 1858, 71 years ago. He discovered that living organisms behave differently with right antipodes than with left. They can assimilate the right-handed antipodes and do not touch the left-handed ones. This is certainly a fact of great importance. According to Curie's principle, he established in this experimental way the dissymmetry of the living organism. Pasteur proved this for yeasts and for some molds. This was observed later for bacteria. This fact is thus established for the two forms of life, for life in the world of molecular phenomena and for that in our world of gravitation.

At first glance, this seems to explain the marked dominance of right antipodes in the production of life.

Yet, in reality this explains nothing, the fundamental problem remains unresolved—why do organisms only assimilate one antipode?

Why does the material of organisms allow right-handed antipodes to penetrate it and not allow left-handed[33] ones?

Taking symmetry as a starting point, Pasteur accepted the possibility of another life in another left-handed space with inverse antipodes—left-handed.

If the observed phenomenon is related to the state of space occupied by life, the right-handed space must, for for reasons currently incomprehensible to us, include the entire solar system, and possibly the galactic system.

Profoundly conscious of the immense impact of his discovery, Pasteur rightly affirmed that he had found an incontestable proof that:

> "molecular dissymmetry, to date the exclusive privilege of products produced under the influence of life, appears as the modifier of physical and chemical phenomena peculiar to the organism."[34]

The ideas of Pasteur have received no response; the facts established by him were not developed.[35]

We have not advanced a single step in the course of these 80 years on the path cleared by Pasteur, we halt, powerless, before the enigmas he brought to light.

We have not done it, although their importance and

---

32. [Works, I, 241.]

33. The translator takes some issue with Vernadsky's statement here, in that it conveys something seemingly absolute which Pasteur did not believe, that is, that life on earth had an exclusively right-handed character. Perhaps it is a mistake, and left and right were unintentionally switched in the text at this point, as today any statement about life's homochirality would state the opposite, that life on Earth has a left-handed character because of its amino acids, which are left-handed. Vernadsky himself said, in his paper *"On the States of Physical Space"*: "Pasteur suggested that in some past period of geological history, *the Solar System had passed through left cosmic space* and that life had originated at that time, and reflected this phenomenon." A cursory reading of several of the cited passages from Pasteur's *Works* makes quite clear that he knew that amino acids, citing albumin specifically, are left-handed, and that sugars, such as tartaric acid which Pasteur famously and frequently studied, are right-handed. Were the text referring only to sugars, such as tartaric acid, it would be a true statement to say that life on Earth has an exclusively right-handed character. It is not known whether Vernadsky took a statement by Pasteur somewhat out of context here, in conveying a right-handed character to all living matter on Earth, or whether it might be a mistake.

34. [Works, II, 1922, 622 (1858).]

35. The following quote from Louis Pasteur very much conveys Vernadsky's message here, that the study of life necessitates a new physics: "You place matter before life and you decide that matter has existed for all eternity. How do you know that the incessant progress of science will not compel scientists to consider that life has existed during eternity, and not matter? You pass from matter to life because your intelligence of today cannot conceive things otherwise. How do you know that in ten thousand years, one will not consider it more likely that matter has emerged from life?" From *Pasteur et la philosophie*, Patrice Pinet, Editions L'Harmattan, p. 63, as cited at: http://en.wikiquote.org/wiki/Louis_Pasteur

the real possibility of studying them experimentally are clear.

This study is important not only for the most complete knowledge of life, but no less for the investigation of the state of physical space in general, because it reveals its new properties which do not appear in any other physical form.

Already, the unique capability of the living organism to distinguish these chemical and physical properties of the environment of life in their relationship with the enantiomorphic vectors is a phenomenon of exclusive importance.

The empirical generalization of Pasteur becomes very interesting today due to the creation of the new physics and the new picture of the Cosmos.

A great number of conclusions accessible to experiment stem from this, on which I cannot however dwell here.

It is important to emphasize the fundamental deduction: the phenomena of life allow us to push the study of the space of the Cosmos further than was possible in any other way. It is the cosmic nature of life which becomes apparent.

Pasteur saw this clearly.

XVI.

Numerous other (related) phenomena have been known in biology for a long time, but were unfortunately not collected and gathered together by systematic scientific thought.

One of these phenomena had already, at the end of the 18th Century, drawn the attention of a French writer, and also a scientist, whose name was then famous: a writer who left a profound imprint on the sentiments and thoughts of men of the 18th Century, a precursor of romanticism on the stage of the last century, Bernardin St. Pierre. He wrote in his *Etudes de la nature* (Studies of Nature),

"It is very remarkable, for example, that all the oceans are full of univalve shells of an infinite number of very different species, who all have their spirals which grow towards to the same side, that is to say, from left to right, as the motion of the earth (globe) when we turn the opening of the shell to the North and towards the Earth. There are only a small number of species that are exceptions and which, for this reason, we call

unique. These forms go from right to left. A direction so general and exceptions which are so particular in the shells must, without a doubt, have their causes in nature and their age in unknown centuries when their germs were created."

Bernardin St. Pierre is more of an artist than a scientist and that being the case he often embraced, with reason and according to his cosmic sentiment of nature, the great phenomenon of life which the experimenter Pasteur approached fifty years after him.

Here, we are approaching an immense domain of facts not yet affected by exact scientific thought.

It is necessary, from now on, to put forward the most important indications which evoke our curiosity. I can only make brief remarks about them here. So first of all, it seems that the directions of seashell spirals of the same species can change in the course of geological time. There does exist, for example, an indica-

Shell of the Fusus antiquus.

tion that the shells of all *Fusus antiquus* of the inferior red sandstone of England (Lower Permian) are all left-handed, whereas the modern ones are all right-handed. If there were no cause—necessarily dissymmetric, according to the principle of Curie—upsetting the symmetry, we would have an equal number of right and left-handed spirals. The cause which determined this phenomenon was thus changed in the course of geological time. It was left enantiomorphic in the given location during the Permian Epoch, and right enantiomorphic during our time.

Drawing of the shell of the Lanistes ovum, a species of African freshwater snail.

The fact that the embryos of mollusks give, in a number of cases, left-handed spirals, whereas the adult forms give right-handed ones indicates, it seems, the possibility of such a change of the space of life.

We stop here, while waiting, powerless, in the face of a need for an explanation of this phenomenon. It is important, above all, to study it and to confirm it. The phenomenon is certainly very complex. Thus, today there are also species of mollusks with left-handed spirals, although their relative number is small when we study them all together.

Moreover, geographic changes are brought to our attention: the *Lanistes* of Lake Tanganyika has left-handed spirals and the same genus, living in the neighboring lakes of Nyassa and Victoria have right-handed spirals. What is the cause of this phenomenon?[36]

Innumerable observations of the same type, gathered together, are scattered throughout the scientific literature, on other spirals of plants and animals which are found everywhere—forms of seeds, of flowers, etc.— Clearly, here we find ourselves in the domain of dissymmetrical phenomena, closely connected with the problems treated by Pasteur, but which are not at all touched upon by theoretical thought.

It is not impossible that in studying these, we will find specific properties of the space connected with life or with unknown dissymmetrical forms.

The work of our current time and of the near future demands that we follow the paths which open up to us.

XVII.

It seems that it is possible to study physical time no less profoundly by research into living phenomena.

The time of the physicist is certainly not the abstract time of the mathematician or the philosopher. Time is manifested in different phenomena under forms which are so different that we had to give it different names in our empirical science. We speak of historical, geological, and cosmic time, etc.

It is convenient to distinguish biological time by the limits in which living phenomena are manifest.

This biological time is now evaluated by $2-3 \times 10^9$

---

36. Lakes Tanganyika, Nysassa (also known as Lake Malawi), and Victoria are all located in eastern Africa, in the regional vicinity of present-day Tanzania. Freshwater snails of the genus *Lanistes* are found in all three lakes, however, as Vernadsky observes here, the shells of those in Lake Tanganyika exhibit left-handed spiral formation, while those in Lakes Nyassa and Victoria are right-handed.

years—by billions of years in the course of which the presence of biological processes known to us in the Cosmos began in the Archaezoic. It is very likely that these years only corresponded to the existence of our planet and not to the duration of life in the Cosmos. Today we arrive at the conclusion that the duration of the existence of celestial bodies in the Cosmos is also limited, that is, that we are, in that case, also dealing with an irreversible process. We ignore the duration of the manifestation of life in the Cosmos, our knowledge of life in the Cosmos being in general minimal. It is possible that billions of years only comprised a very small part of biological time.

For life on Earth, the irreversible process is expressed within the limits of this time by the evolution of species.

From the point of view of time, it is probably a manifestation of Redi's principle, that is to say the succession of generations, which must be considered as a fundamental phenomenon.

We have a number of phenomena in this succession of generations accessible to quantitative study and which give an exact, mathematical and quantitative representation of the structure of the polar vector, which corresponds geometrically to the processes of evolution.

Unfortunately, the scientific facts related to it are dispersed and not always exact. Today, we can only evaluate the constants of biological time by the limits of numbers and not by the numbers themselves. But the change in our ideas about the position of life in the Cosmos urgently requires the organization of systematic experimental investigations in this direction.

The irrefutable existence of *a minimum limit of the duration of the succession of generations* is quite obvious. This limit indicates the minimum time necessary for the formation of a determined number of organisms, that is, not only for the formation of their mechanisms, but also for all their most complex chemical structures—albumins, etc. This phenomenon is clearly submitted to determined laws.

I tried elsewhere to establish that this limit corresponds to the duration of the minimum average division of the unicellular organism and is carried out with an intensity reaching the limit which is physically possible.

The limit is not placed there by the short duration of the succession of generations, insufficient for the formation of innumerable and complex chemical

Depicted here is a model of the geological time scale with the evolution of life on Earth divided into its various eras and periods. Vernadsky saw the consistent upward evolution of life as a unique characteristic of biological time.

compositions necessary for life, but by the properties of the physical environment and moreover by the properties of gas, by the respiration of organisms. The organism must carry out its gaseous exchange in such a way that its living environment is not destroyed. Thus the speed of the propagation of its geochemical energy by reproduction (the succession of generations) cannot exceed the speed of the sound wave in a gaseous medium, in which the organism breathes.

The fact that life can actually reach this limit proves the extreme intensity of the living process which is clearly connected, but not exclusively, with the properties of the material medium.

The research of this limit is on the agenda. As far as we can judge, the minimum duration for the succession of generations is somewhere between 16 and 22 minutes, closer to 20 minutes it seems. This length requires an exact determination. It is an important biological constant. It can play the role of a natural unit for the study of biological time. We can consider it as a measure of biological time. Its determination does not seem to pose experimental difficulty.

It appears that there is also a maximum limit for the

Vernadsky viewed the power of man's mind as a geological force of unprecedented magnitude, saying: "The intelligence of man begins to manifest itself today in the process of the biosphere, always more clearly and decisively, and changes the established geoplogical process in a radical manner." Pictured here are two satellite images, before and after the construction of the Three Gorges Dam on the Yangtze River in China, the largest power generation station in the world.

succession of generations. In some vegetable organisms, we observe that it corresponds to several hundreds of years, that is to say 10^7, maybe 10^8 minutes. Its determination is also a matter of time.

Thus the amplitude of the variations of the succession of generations is very significant and can vary by millions or tens of millions.

The change of the duration of generations in the process of evolution, in the course of geological time, is very characteristic of biological time. We will not have an idea of this process and its character until there is a concentration of a sufficient quantity of facts. For man, the duration of a generation in the process of evolution seems to grow in the course of time.

The phenomenon must be studied on the basis of the new physics in the complex "Space-Time." The Space of life has, as we have seen, a particular symmetrical state which is unique in nature. The time which corresponds to it not only has the character of polar vectors, but a particular parameter, proper to itself, a particular unit of measure, connected with life.

I cannot dwell any longer on these phenomena. It is only important to me to make their importance known.

A multitude of problems suddenly appear; the possibility of a quantitative scientific investigation is clear.

It is not until after the facts which have been known for a long time become systematized or that new facts become amassed that we will be able to realize what this will contribute to the study of biological time in connection with the succession of living generations which characterizes it.

XVIII.

But it is clear, from the standpoint of the problem which interests us here,—that of the importance of the investigation of life for the construction of the scientific picture of the Universe,—that this investigation is of interest for the space and time of the Universe. It introduces new traits, not known from other physical or chemical phenomena.

It is clear that life cannot be separated from the Cosmos, and that its study must have an impact—perhaps very significant—on scientific representation.

This does not only concern space and time, but also other fundamental elements of the Cosmos. I can only indicate them here.

Thus, life is set almost entirely apart from other phenomena in regards to the energetics in the Universe, in diminishing and never increasing its entropy. According to the opinion of Prof. Jaeger, life creates, through the evolutionary process, forms which are increasingly lacking in elements of symmetry. Finally, the intelligence of man begins to manifest itself today in the process of the biosphere, always more clearly and decisively, and changes the established geological process in a radical manner.

The new representations of the Universe created by the new physics compels us to pay special attention to the study of the phenomena of life which indicate their character which is not only terrestrial, but *cosmic*.

It is especially important because of the biological problems which suddenly arise, and which can be encompassed by number and measurement, the fundamental approach, leading to the construction of the scientific Universe.

Vast new horizons of research thus open themselves up to biology. The scientific confirmation of the fact that life is not a planetary phenomenon, but rather cosmic, will have immense consequences for biological and humanitarian conceptions.

The future will decide whether this is the case. But as we wait, the development of the new physics allows us to follow not the way of philosophical constructions, always insufficient and precarious, but that of exact scientific research, based on number and measurement. The new way which has been cleared before us, will lead us, perhaps far from the biosphere, in which today the entire work of the biologist, and to a lesser degree that of the geochemist, is concentrated.

V. Vernadsky
**Member of the Academy of
Sciences of Leningrad
Correspondent of the Institut de France**

A Vernadskian Reconsideration of Galactic Cycles and Evolution

by Benjamin Deniston

May 16—As has been emphasized recently by Lyndon LaRouche and his *Executive Intelligence Review* magazine and LaRouche Political Action Committee, to understand climate, weather, and the behavior of water on our planet, we must start by understanding the role of our galaxy.[1]

Records of the largest climate variations over the past half billion years correspond to changes in the galactic environment experienced by our Solar System—indicating that the galaxy has the strongest role in determining the climate variations on Earth.[2]

The implications of this can be looked at in two ways.

On the one side, an adherent to the modern school of scientific reductionism may see this as, perhaps, an interesting phenomenon, but one with no general impact on our understanding of the nature and ordering of causality in the universe.

On the other side, a mind which is not suffering from the debilitating effects of the destruction of science led by David Hilbert and Bertrand Russell[3] (mathematical reductionism) will see this as a clue to defining a new un-

Yuri Beletsky, August 2010

One of the European Southern Observatory's telescopes in their Very Large Telescope array uses a laser beam to create an artificial star high in the Earth's atmosphere, allowing the astronomers to correct for atmospheric distortion (utilizing adaptive optics) as they study the central regions of our Milky Way Galaxy.

derstanding of the hierarchical nature of causality in the universe—pursuing the conception of science defined by Nicolas of Cusa (as in his 1440 *De Docta Ignorantia*) and his follower Johannes Kepler.

Here, we will take the opportunity of the publication of the first English translation of Vladimir Vernadsky's 1930 report, "The Study of Life and the New Physics," to examine another clue, again pointing us towards the need for a higher understanding of our galaxy.[4]

Studies have shown that there are cycles in the evolutionary development of animal life over the past 540 million years on Earth—cycles which correspond in period and in phase to cyclical aspects of the motion of our Solar System through our galaxy.

This can also be looked at in two ways.

1. In the modern domination of Russellian reductionism, a "kill mechanism" is sought to explain how different galactic environments can accelerate the extinction rate of species and, thereby, imprint records of these cosmic fluctuations in the evolutionary record.

2. For an approach freed from the disease of reductionism, we can instead look to the views of Vernadsky, as presented in his 1930 report, "The Study of Life and the New Physics."

A student of Dmitri Mendeleev, and an avid opponent to the influence of Bertrand Russell on Russian and Soviet science, Vernadsky's hypotheses about life in the Cosmos provide an important basis to investigate the re-

1. "New Perspectives on the Western Water Crisis," *EIR*, April 3, 2015; "Galactic Man: Shadow versus Principle," *EIR*, May 15, 2015; and the LaRouchePAC water page, at www.larouchepac.com/global-water
2. See "Celestial driver of Phanerozoic climate?" Nir Shaviv and Ján Veizer, *GSA Today*, July 2003.
3. For more on the destructive role of Hilbert and Russell, see Jason Ross's presentation to the May 16, 2015 Schiller Institute New York City conference, and "The Escape from Hilbert's 'ZETA' 'X': Mapping the Cosmos!" by Lyndon LaRouche, *EIR*, March 19, 2010.
4. See "The Study of Life and the New Physics," in this issue of *EIR*.

lationship between the changing expression of life on Earth and the subsuming galactic system.

This provides another avenue for understanding that which subsumes our Solar System, our Earth, and the processes therein.

Identifying the Important Evidence

Fossil records leave a map of the evolutionary development of complex life on Earth, showing an overall increase in the number of distinct animal species (and more clearly in measures of genera) on the plant over the past 540 million years (as is best recorded in records of ocean life). However, upon this overall increase is imprinted a smaller periodic rise and fall in the number of genera at any given time. Early indication of this go back to the 1980s,[5] but more recent analysis (with a more complete fossil record) has solidified the evidence for a cycle in the decline and increase in the number of genera over time[6] (see **Figure 1**). Perhaps most interestingly, this cycle corresponds with the period and phase of cyclical aspects of the motion of our Solar System through the Milky Way Galaxy.

Existing attempts to explain this correlation between galactic activity and evolution of life rely upon a sequence of domino-like effects resulting from the introduction of a "kill mechanism." They look for ways that cosmic processes might kill off large enough numbers of individual animals (either directly, or by creating certain environmental effects which will do so), which, in turn, could then lead to extinctions of entire species; and, if the killing rate were powerful enough and sustained, then to the extinctions of large numbers of different species, resulting in the extinctions of entire genera, and then families, culminating in a "mass extinction."[7]

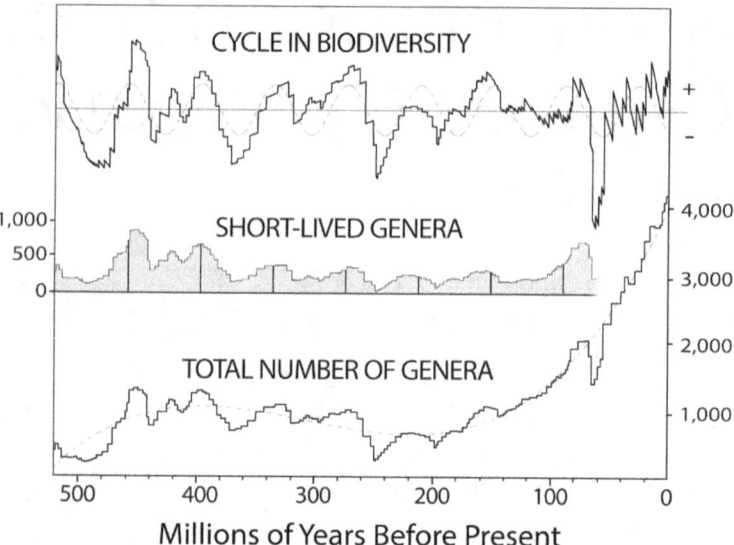

FIGURE 1
Marine Fossil Diversity

adapted from Rohde & Muller, 2005

The belief that increased extinction rates, or even mass extinctions can be explained by this type of a bottom-up causality is not a demonstrated generalization based on evidence, but, rather, the product of certain reductionist beliefs and assumptions. In reality, the phenomena of mass extinctions are still poorly understood.[8] What we know from the fossil record is that there can be relatively rapid—in geological terms—transitions where many species, genera, and families disappear from the record and are replaced by new forms—although these more dramatic (and rapid) shifts exist within the context of an already ongoing slower turnover rate. How and why this occurred the way it did is still not well understood.

So, rather than assuming we must accept a reductionist framework, here we will take a different approach.

Perhaps most important for this shift in approach is

5. "Periodic Extinction of Families and Genera," Raup and Sepkoski, 1986, *Science,* Vol. 231, Issue 4740.

6. "Cycles in fossil diversity," Rohde and Muller, March 10, 2005, *Nature,* Vol. 434.

7. The initial attempt to define such a kill mechanism posits that high-energy radiation experienced in different parts of the galaxy damages and kills more animals when the Solar System is in these regions, leading to greater extinction rates ("Do extragalactic cosmic rays induce cycles in fossil diversity?" Medvedev and Melott, 2007). In a more recent attempt to explain this correlation, another scientist proposed that the extinctions are the product of comet impacts with the Earth, produced periodically by the Solar System's cyclical passage through more dense regions of the galaxy (at which times, comets hiding in the outskirts of our Solar System can have their orbits perturbed, sending some towards the inner planets). See, "Disc dark matter in the Galaxy and potential cycles of extraterrestrial impacts, mass extinctions and geo-

logical events," Michael R. Rampino, Feb. 18, 2015, *Monthly Notices of the Royal Astronomical Society,* Vol. 448, Issue 2.

8. For example, a rather thorough 2006 paper by Richard Bambach re-analyzed what is known about extinctions and mass extinctions over the past 540 million years. His last two conclusions were interesting. "Mass extinctions are diverse and vary in intensity, selectivity, and timing. They are not homogeneous in effect or in cause." And, "Knowledge of timing and of geographic and environmental distribution of effects is inadequate. At this time, no consensus on proximate cause of death has been obtained for any extinction event." See, "Phanerozoic Biodiversity Mass Extinctions," Richard K. Bambach, *Annual Review of Earth and Planetary Sciences,* Vol. 34 (May 2006), pp. 127-155.

Fossilized remains of an extinct species of sea stars (Dipsacaster africanus) from around 130 million years ago. The fossils were discovered in Taba, Morocco.

to recognize that it isn't simply extinctions which define these cycles, but extinctions and originations (the generation of new species, genera, and families).

As stated in a 2013 paper on the subject by Melott and Bambach, the evidence for a cycle in the process of the evolutionary development of life on Earth "results from the coherent interaction of both extinction and origination fluctuations, producing a stronger signal than either would or could alone."[9] So we must also ask why there exist periodic phases characterized by the origination of new genera.

Put simply, we're looking for more than a kill mechanism. We're examining, on the one side, the anti-entropic development of life on Earth, and, on the other, the relation of our Solar System to our galactic system—and we're asking why cycles in both processes correlate so well. The work of Vernadsky provides a new basis to investigate this relation, in these top-down terms.

Vernadsky's 'Study of Life and the New Physics'

We don't know what life is.

Vernadsky's work provides an important distinction between the study of living processes and life per se. We can study living processes as effects of life, as particular expressions of life, without assuming that these specific expressions, alone, define life per se. This important distinction provides the needed framework to properly pursue the properties and characteristics of life, per se—investigating that which underlies certain particular expressions and manifestations.

Vernadsky took up exactly this approach in his 1930 report, "The Study of Life and the New Physics." Examining the identifiable properties of living processes—as they can be studied in the context of their existence in the biogeochemical medium of the Earth's biosphere—he separated the properties into two lists:

First, those properties which are associated with the planetary (biogeochemical) medium within which living processes are manifested on Earth.

Second, those properties displayed by living processes which can not be attributed to the characteristics and properties of this planetary context, and, thus, might express something more universal about life, per se.[10]

Vernadsky immediately follows this second list with a conclusion which will be upsetting to today's reductionists: "This list is not complete, but it indicates, with evidence, that life manifests itself in the Cosmos in other forms than those which biology normally displays."

Since living processes are not merely a phenomenon of geochemistry[11]—but are an expression of a principle of life, per se, manifested in the context of a geochemical medium—we should be willing to seek out in the Cosmos, other expressions of these non-planetary properties of life.

Vernadsky then dedicates the entire latter half of his report to the two non-planetary properties of life, which he thinks could be the most fruitful in investigating how "life manifests itself in the Cosmos in other forms than those which biology normally displays."

"Here, I will dwell upon two phenomena which will allow for the clarification of the important role which the investigation of life plays in the scientific picture of the Universe, created by the new physics, notably upon the dissymmetry of the space of living organisms and on biological time. In the first case, this is a matter of new properties (a particular state of physical space), observed in living organisms, and in the second, new properties of physical time.[12]"

9. "Analysis of periodicity of extinction using the 2012 geological timescale," Melott and Bambach, 2013; citing, "A ubiquitous ~62-Myr periodic fluctuation superimposed on general trends in fossil biodiversity. II. Evolutionary dynamics associated with periodic fluctuation in marine diversity," Melott and Bambach, 2011, *Paleobiology.*

10. See section 10 of "The Study of Life and the New Physics."
11. Despite the delusions of Vernadsky's opponent and adversary, Alexander Oparin. See, "A.I. Oparin: Fraud, Fallacy, or Both?" by Meghan Rouillard, Spring 2013 issue of *21st Century Science & Technology.*
12. See section 11 of "The Study of Life and the New Physics."

In his 18-section report, Vernadsky focuses most of the latter half to the first of these two, "the dissymmetry of the space of living organisms" (sections 11-16), followed by one section on biological time (section 17).

Vernadsky's work—both distinguishing a principle of life, per se, from the particular expressions of living processes we're familiar with on Earth, and positing the need to investigate other potential expressions of this principle in the Cosmos—provides a critical, non-reductionist basis for investigating the correlation of cycles of extinction and origination in the fossil record with the cycles of our Solar System's motion through our galaxy—that is, to investigate the potential relationship between the process of the anti-entropic development of living processes on Earth, and the processes of the cosmic system of our galaxy.

As we will see, Vernadsky's conception of dissymmetrical states of space will be key.

Cosmic Dissymmetry

In a different address (delivered one year later), Vernadsky made some interesting remarks specifically regarding galactic systems. Citing early studies examining the distribution of "spiral nebulae" (as spiral galaxies used to be called), Vernadsky hypothesized their orientations could be an expression of a "dissymmetrical" characteristic of the Cosmos.

"The spiral form of nebulae and of some stellar agglomerations indicates the probable presence of analogous dissymmetrical phenomena in the Cosmos. If the right spirals predominate in effect, clearly, among the spiral nebulae, as numerous photographs attest, or in certain parts of the universe, right spiral nebulae are concentrated, and in others left spiral nebulae, the existence of dissymmetric spaces in the Cosmos would become more than probable. This dissymmetry would seem to be analogous to that which we observe in the space penetrated by life, that is to say, that it possesses enantiomorphic vectors and both of the vectors—left and right—could exist there at the same time, but not in equal number; the right-handed vectors most often predominate there.[13]"

While recent studies indicate Vernadsky may have been onto something interesting regarding the large-scale distribution of galaxies,[14] here we're interested in the potential dissymmetrical characteristics of a single galaxy—our own.

For a single spiral galaxy to express an inherent dissymmetry—i.e., to have an inherent handedness—there has to be a physical distinction between the top and bottom (north and south),[15] a distinction expressing the global characteristics of the galactic system as a whole.

Most importantly, if we are working from Vernadsky's conception of potential cosmic expressions of a quality of dissymmetrical space which we see expressed in living organisms, then perhaps the top-bottom (north-south) distinction which defines the dissymmetry of a spiral galaxy should be expressed in the response of living processes most strongly. That is, it would make sense that the most important evidence for defining an inherently dissymmetrical space of a galaxy would be the reaction of living processes to the influence of that dissymmetrical space.

Holding that thought, let's return to what we know about the relationship of our Solar System to the galaxy.

As we orbit around the center of our galaxy, the Solar System also passes above and below the galactic plane, in a bobbing-type motion. Based on current measurements and analysis, the cycles of this up-and-down-motion are roughly 30 (26-37) million years from mid-plane, through a peak, back to mid-plane, or 30 million years from one peak to the opposite peak, or 60 million years from one peak, through the opposite, and back to the same side (see **Figure 2**).

Most researchers think that the conditions north or south of the galactic plane should be generally similar,

ies) Vernadsky was referring to in 1931, 80 years later, a professor from the University of Michigan, Michael Longo, published a study showing that there is indeed a preferred orientation to spiral galaxies, depending on which direction one looks. Using a data set of 260,000 clearly defined spiral galaxies, Longo found that in a specific direction (about 10° from the spin axis of our own galaxy), we see more left-handed spiral galaxies than right-handed ones. In a following study, looking from the Southern Hemisphere (instead of the Northern), Longo showed that, in the exact opposite direction, the opposite is the case: There are more right-handed galaxies are seen than left-handed ones. This is a remarkable finding, one we can be sure Vernadsky would find highly significant. See "Detection of a Dipole in the Handedness of Spiral Galaxies with Redshifts z ~0.04," by Michael J. Longo, *Physics Letters B*, 699, pp. 224-229 (2011).

15. Otherwise, a spiral galaxy which appears to be right-handed when being observed from one side would, at the same time, appear to be left-handed when observed from the other side. The left vs. right distinction would merely be a product of the location of observation, not an intrinsic expression of the galactic system itself, unless something distinguished one side from the other.

13. From Vernadsky's 1931 speech, "On the Conditions of the Appearance of Life on Earth," translated from French by Meghan Rouillard,
14. Although it is unclear exactly which "spiral nebulae" (spiral galax-

FIGURE 2

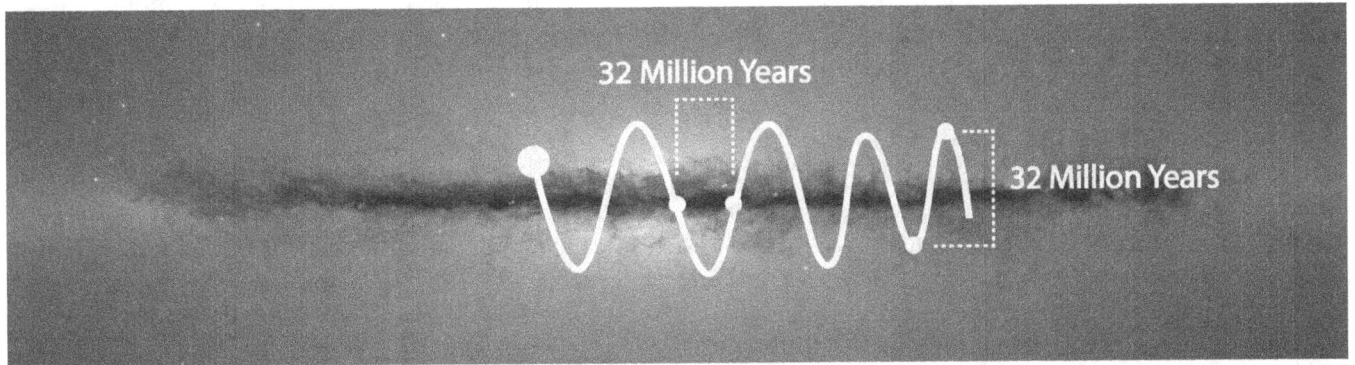

NASA, ESA, & Hubble Heritage Team (STScI/AURA)

Variations in the climate, the temperature, corresponding to the motion of our Solar System, above and below the galactic plane are shown here.

and, therefore, any imprint of this changing galactic environment recorded in the Earth's history should express a 30-million-year periodicity.

In fact this is true for at least one abiotic process, the climate, where a 30-million-year cycle has been found.[16]

However, records of the evolutionary development of life on Earth display a ~62-million-year fluctuation.[17] As mentioned above, this biodiversity cycle appears strongest when one is not only examining extinctions, but extinctions together with originations (the appearance of new genera), a pairing which forces the investigation beyond the reductionist's search for a kill mechanism.

Thus, the evidence for a relationship between processes of our galactic system, and the evolutionary development of life on Earth, is not simply associated with being either above or below the galactic plane, but with the characteristics of one side vs. the other. Within the reductionist camp, this is taken as evidence to doubt the existence of a connection between this galactic process and the evolution of living processes on Earth (despite the clear correlation), because the reductionists have no reason to hypothesize a distinction between the north and south sides.[18] But when viewed

from the conceptions of Vernadsky, the distinction which serves as their basis for doubt becomes our point of interest.

A physical distinction between one side of the galaxy and the other is required for our Vernadskian hypothesis of a dissymmetrical characteristic governing the physical space of the galactic system—providing the critical evidence needed to define a distinct, intrinsic handedness of the system (irrespective of one's vantage point).

The evolutionary cycle being 60 million years, rather than 30 (and matching the proper phase), provides the needed evidence for a distinction, indicating the potential for an inherent difference in the north vs. south sides of our galaxy, and, thereby, its inherent dissymmetry. It is most appropriate that fluctuations in the history of the evolutionary development of living processes on Earth are what provide the critical evidence for defining an intrinsic dissymmetry of our galactic system—indicating galactic manifestation of dissymmetrical space, to which living processes on Earth are responsive.[19]

Space-Time of Anti-Entropy

In the terminology and framework pursued by Vernadsky, this could be an expression of a dissymmetrical

16. See "Is the Solar System's Galactic Motion Imprinted in the Phanerozoic Climate?" by Nir Shaviv, Andreas Prokoph, and Ján Veizer; *Scientific Reports*, Article number: 6150 doi:10.1038/srep06150, published Aug. 21, 2014.

17. Indications of other cycles have also been identified, but this one is clear and unambiguous, as stated in the initial paper identifying its existence, "…the 62-Myr cycle is not a subtle signal. It is evident even in the raw data, dominant in the short-lived genera and strongly confirmed by statistical analysis." See "Cycles in fossil diversity," Rohde and Muller, March 10, 2005, *Nature*, Vol. 434.

18. For example, "The Sun currently oscillates up and down across the Galactic plane every 52-74 [million years], but plausible responses

would seem to occur every mid-plane crossing (namely 26-37Myr)" (Rohde, Muller; "Cycles in fossil diversity," 2005); and "Thus, these ~60 Ma periodicities are probably unrelated to the 32 Ma cycle discussed here, unless there is a very large north-south asymmetry relative to the galactic plane" (Shaviv, Prokoph, Veizer, "Is the Solar System's Galactic Motion Imprinted in the Phanerozoic Climate?" 2014).

19. Recall how Vernadsky was calling for investigating how "life manifests itself in the Cosmos in other forms than those which biology normally displays."

space-time characteristics of our galactic system.[20]

This is not the first indication that the study of galactic systems could require a new conception of a self-bounded space-time intrinsic to that galactic system.[21] However, Vernadsky's direction of work indicates that we should open our minds to the qualities of the space-time characteristics of living processes (rather than simply abiotic physics), if we are to truly attempt to understand the Cosmos as containing a principle of life, per se, and galactic systems therein.

With this evidence for a relation between the evolutionary development of life on Earth and the processes of our galactic system, we see the option to invert the investigation—to examine the characteristics expressed by evolution as informing us about the nature of our galactic system as a whole.

As Vernadsky correctly identified in his 1926 address on evolution,[22] there is an intrinsic direction in the evolutionary development of life on Earth—the increasing energy-flux density of the biosphere system—which Vernadsky called his "second biogeochemical principle":

This biogeochemical principle which I will call the second biogeochemical principle can be formulated thus: The evolution of species, leading to the creation of new, stable, living forms, must move in the direction of an increasing of the biogenic migration of atoms in the biosphere....

[This second biogeochemical principle] indicates, in my opinion, with an infallible logic, the existence of a determined direction, in the sense of how the processes of evolution must necessarily take place.... All theories of evolution must take into consideration the existence of this determined direction of the process of evolution, which, with the subsequent developments in science, will be able to be numerically evaluated. It seems impossible to me, for several reasons, to speak of evolutionary theories without taking into account the fundamental question of the existence of a determined direction, invariable in the processes of evolution, in the course of all the geological epochs. Taken together, the annals of paleontology do not show the character of a chaotic upheaval, sometimes in one direction, sometimes in another, but of phenomena, for which the development is carried out in a determined manner, always in the same direction, in that of the increasing of consciousness, of thought, and of the creation of forms augmenting the action of life on the ambient environment.[23]

Since Vernadsky's time, we've accumulated a much larger and more detailed map of the evolutionary development of life. While the new evidence strongly conforms to Vernadsky's second biogeochemical principle,[24] we are still far from understanding the principle which has composed that map.

In pursuit of this, we've been pointed to the processes of our own galactic system—as the macroevolutionary pulsations associated with the anti-entropic development of living processes on Earth beat in harmony with our Solar System's experience of the dissymmetrical characteristics of our galaxy.

Rather than simply an Earth-based phenomenon, the development of life on Earth could be an expression of an anti-entropic character of our galaxy, returning us to the opening challenge: understanding the causal role of our galactic system in the hierarchical ordering of the Universe.

20. Vernadsky often focused on, and returned to the space-time properties of living processes as critical to investigating and understanding life phenomena. He developed the need to consider the space-time of living processes as dissymmetrical with a polar vector. This is the case in the cited paper, "Life and the New Physics," as well as other works, emphatically his series on the Problems of Biogeochemistry, available in "150 Years of Vernadsky: The Biosphere," *21st Century Science & Technology,* Jason Ross (Editor), Meghan Rouillard (Series Editor).

21. Observational evidence indicating discrepant redshift measurements for galactic systems (i.e., redshift values which can not be attributed to any currently accepted cause of redshifts, such as cosmological expansion, recessional velocity, or relativistic effects), can (although highly controversial) be taken as possible evidence for unique space-time characteristics distinct to an individual galactic system (see *Quasars, Redshifts and Controversies,* Halton Arp, 1988, Cambridge University Press). Also the "M-sigma relation" (showing that the mass of a galaxy's bulge scales in a very tight proportion to the mass of a phenomenon often referred to as the supermassive black hole at the center of that same galaxy) indicates a higher structure and coherence to a galactic system as a unity. These (and other provocative lines of evidence) tickle the imagination to ponder the yet-to-be-discovered principle organizing the existence and development of a galactic system.

22. "The Evolution of Species and Living Matter," 1926, translated from French by Meghan Rouillard,

23. This second biogeochemical principle should also be considered as a non-planetary property of life, according to Vernadsky's analysis in his "Study of Life Phenomena and the New Physics."

24. For example, see, "Macro-Ecological Revolutions: Mass Extinctions as Shadows of Anti-Entropic Growth," Benjamin Deniston, *EIR,* March 23, 2012.

Hersh Revelations Can Sink Obama, Bush, and the Saudis

by Jeffrey Steinberg

May 18—Noted investigative journalist Seymour Hersh just penned a ten thousand-word exposé of the Obama Administration's fraudulent account of the killing of Osama bin Laden. Obama and his White House coterie of spin-meisters have just suffered another serious blow. Beyond that, the Hersh revelations have once again shined a spotlight on the prominent role of the Saudi monarchy in promoting and protecting international jihadist terrorism.

In a recent interview with the Real News Network, author Hersh revealed that the Saudi monarchy had paid an undisclosed, but significant amount of money, to the Pakistani government to keep Osama bin Laden under quasi-house arrest in Abbottabad, a Pakistani city dominated by major military facilities, from 2006 until his assassination by U.S. Seal Team 6 in May 2011. The Saudis insisted that the Americans must be kept in the dark about bin Laden's whereabouts. Some leading circles in the Saudi Royal Family were apparently terrified that the Americans would get their hands on bin Laden, and learn the full story about the Kingdom's role in the September 11, 2001 attacks.

Pressure has been mounting for President Obama to finally declassify the 28-page chapter from the report of the Joint Congressional Inquiry into 9/11, which documented some of the evidence that leading figures within the Saudi royal family, including the then-Saudi Ambassador to Washington, Prince Bandar bin Sultan, had bankrolled the 9/11 hijackers. President George W. Bush had originally classified the entire 28-page chapter, to protect the Saudis and conceal his own close personal ties to Prince Bandar. During his 2008 Presidential campaign, and on at least two subsequent occasions, Obama had promised 9/11 family members that he would declassify the chapter, but he has so far steadfastly refused to keep his promise.

LPAC

Former Senator Bob Graham speaks at a January 7, 2015 press conference in Washington, D.C., along with Congressmen Jones and Lynch, and family members of the 9/11 victims.

The demand for declassification has been led by former Sen. Bob Graham (D-Fla.), who chaired the original Joint Congressional Inquiry into 9/11. Members of the U.S. House of Representatives, led by Rep. Walter Jones (R-N.C.), Stephen Lynch (D-Mass.), and Thomas Massie (R-Ky.) have introduced legislation in the last and current sessions of Congress to declassify the pages, and have held a series of high-profile news conferences to press the case. A Federal judge in Florida is now reviewing 86,000 pages of suppressed FBI files, further detailing the links of leading Saudi Royals to the 9/11 hijackers.

The Hersh revelations, that the assassination of bin Laden was the result of evidence provided by a walk-in former Pakistani military official, and that the killing raid was carried out with the full cooperation of top Pakistani military officials, has triggered a firestorm in Washington, where the Obama Administration has attempted desperately to discredit Hersh's account, but to no avail.

White House/Pete Souza

The White House Situation Room on May 1, 2011, while the operation against Osama bin Laden was in process.

A Clumsy Coverup

What the Hersh story reveals is a clumsy, lying cover-up by top Obama Administration officials, including the President himself. Among the key Hersh findings: Pakistani military authorities facilitated the raid on the bin Laden compound, to the point that the security guards, provided by Pakistan's Inter-Services Intelligence (ISI), were withdrawn from the compound prior to the U.S. raid, and Pakistani air defenses were shut down to allow the two U.S. special operations helicopters to cross the border and travel over 100 miles through Pakistani airspace to reach the Abbottabad compound. President Obama violated the deal that had been made with Pakistan's two top military commanders, then-Chief of Staff Gen. Ashfaq Pervez Kayani and then-ISI Director General Ahmad Shuja Pasha, in arranging the bin Laden execution. It had been agreed that the U.S. would claim that bin Laden had been killed in a drone raid in Afghanistan, thus protecting and concealing the active collusion of the Pakistani authorities.

On cue, the Obama Administration and allied news organizations have taken the bait and launched a campaign of lies to discredit the Hersh account.

Between the continuing demands for the release of the Joint Inquiry chapter, and the controversy swelling around the Hersh accounts of the bin Laden killing, the role of Saudi Arabia in financing global jihadist terrorism has once again bubbled to the surface.

Hersh's charges that the Saudis paid Pakistan to keep bin Laden under comfortable lock and key—and out of the reach of American authorities—add further weight to the demand that the full truth about the persistent Saudi role in the bankrolling of terrorism come out.

The Ugly Truth

In a January 2015 Capitol Hill press conference, Senator Graham, flanked by Representatives Jones and Lynch and representatives of the 9/11 families, warned that, so long as the suppressed truth about the Saudi role in 9/11 remained under wraps, the United States would be vulnerable to another devastating terror attack, and groups like the Islamic State would grow and spread internationally.

To provide you, the reader, with some further details of the known involvement of leading Saudi officials, financial institutions, and royals, in the spreading of jihadist terror, and to detail some of the most significant links between the Saudi and British monarchies in this effort, *EIR* presents the third installment[1] of a series of dossiers on the financial roots of global jihadist terror.

---

1. "Charles of Arabia: The British Monarchy, Saudi Arabia, & 9/11," *EIR*, May 23, 2014; and "King Faisal and the Forging of the Anglo-Saudi Terror Alliance," *EIR*, June 27, 2014.

British-Saudi Bank Cartel Alleged To Finance Terrorism

by Richard Freeman and Jeffrey Steinberg

May 17—Seymour Hersh's recent expose showing that Osama Bin Laden had been under house arrest in Pakistan since 2006, and was being financed heavily in this situation by the Saudis, once again highlights Saudi sponsorship of Bin Laden and al-Qaeda. Since September 11, 2001 various parts of the U.S. government, including individuals in the executive branch and intelligence agencies, and members of Congress, together with the 9/11 victims' families, have repeatedly sought to expose the Saudi role in terrorism.

Their efforts have been turned back by both the Bush and Obama Administrations, based on the claim that an alliance with Wahhabi religious zealots, with views which never escaped the Seventh Century B.C., is so important to U.S. national security interests, that it must be protected at all costs. In the Bush case, there is a direct and longstanding Bush family business and political alliance with Saudi Arabia and Kuwait and their British controllers. The Bushes also share, with the House of Windsor, a geopolitical strategy which preserves the hegemony of the Anglo-American monetarists, while reducing the world's population by any means necessary, including wars and famines. The Saudis played a major role in the defeat of the Russians in Afghanistan, in the wars against Russian interests in the Balkans and Bosnia, and play a significant role in continuing terrorism against Russia and China, and the genocidal population wars which have engulfed the entire Middle East, Africa, and South Asia.

Obama, never anything more than a Wall Street, City of London pawn, has continued Bush's policies.

This is the third in the *EIR* series exposing Saudi Arabia's role in terrorism and its financing. Here we will outline some of the accusations which have been made, repeatedly, against related Saudi-controlled banking institutions, by members of the U.S. government, other governments, and independent researchers. Most critically, we will also show that the individuals involved in these related institutions have longstanding and deep relationships to the House of Windsor, specifically through Prince Charles. Prince Philip, Charles's father, is, like Charles, a fanatical Malthusian, once stating that he would like to be reincarnated as a deadly virus in order to achieve radical population reduction.

Saudi Arabia and the House of Windsor

Queen Elizabeth sent Prince Charles on his first official state visit to Saudi Arabia in 1986, at the age of 38; he made his eleventh state visit in February 10-11,

White House/Pete Souza

Barack Obama and George W. Bush on Air Force One, December 9, 2013.

2015. During that last visit, Charles had a private meeting with King Salman that covered wide-ranging strategic affairs; after that tete-a-tete, King Salman threw a lavish luncheon in Charles's honor, attended by over 50 Saudi royals, featuring most prominently the powerful Prince Mohammed bin Salman al-Saud, the King's son, who is Defense Minister and was recently named Deputy Crown Prince, the number-two heir to the Saudi throne. Charles also met with former Crown Prince Muqrin, and his old friend Prince Turki al-Faisal bin Abdulaziz al-Saud, who for a quarter of a century was head of Saudi Intelligence. Charles was given access and a reception greater than that accorded to any head of state.

Charles has been accused of being a road-block to investigations into the financing and control of international terrorism pursued by the families of the victims of the 9/11 attack. Authors Mark Hollingsworth and Sandy Mitchell documented and wrote in the book, *Saudi Babylon: Torture, Corruption and Cover-Up Inside the House of Saud,* that, "Prince Charles' relationships with prominent members of the House of Saud have created serious problems and obstacles to UK agencies investigating claims of Saudi financing of international terrorism, according to Special Branch sources."

Charles has also been at the center of securing major British deals to supply sophisticated weapons to the Saudis, including the al-Yamamah II deal of the late 1980s and 1990s, and the al-Salam deal, under which the Saudis purchased 72 Typhoon Eurofighter aircraft. He clinched it during his Feb. 17-19, 2014 state visit to Saudi Arabia, after British Prime Minister David Cameron had utterly failed to conclude such a deal.

The Oxford Centre for Islamic Studies (OCIS), based at Oxford University, appears to be a central command point for Charles's working with individuals whom, alternately, governments, lawsuits, books, and articles, have named as leaders in international terrorism, including the 9/11 attack. Charles was an enthusiastic supporter of the Centre from its 1985 inception, and when the Queen appointed him its royal patron in 1993, he took it over.

The Oxford Centre for Islamic Studies

Examine just four of the Centre's leaders and funders:

• **Abdullah Omar Naseef.** Naseef has been chair-

creative commons/David Hawgood

The Oxford Centre for Islamic Studies

man of the Board of Trustees of the Oxford Centre for a decade, and perhaps much longer (annual reports of the Centre are hard to obtain). Born in Jeddah, Saudi Arabia, in 1939, Naseef apparently helped set up and preside over terrorist networks at a much higher level than Osama bin Laden.

In 1962, according to his curriculum vitae, Naseef helped create the terrorist-sponsoring, Riyadh-based Wahhabite Muslim World League (MWL); in 1983, he became its chairman, a post he would hold until 1993.

In 1983-84, Naseef appointed Abdullah Azzam as the MWL's Education Department head, and, through Azzam, helped to create the organization called the Khidamat al-Maktab, the chief support organization of the Mujahiddin. *In 1989, keeping every one of its core functions, the Khidamat changed its name to al-Qaeda.* That is, Naseef helped found the organization that today is al-Qaeda. Respected author Ahmed Rashid, in his book *Taliban: Militant Islam, Oil and Fundamentalism in Central Asia*, reported,

The centre for the Arab-Afghans [the Afghansi mujahideen who were born outside Afghanistan, but fought Russian troops in Afghanistan—ed.] was the offices of the World Muslim League and the Muslim Brotherhood in Peshawar [Pakistan], which was run by Abdullah Azzam," who worked for, and was directed by, Abdullah Naseef.

Rasheed explained that that money flowed into Naseef's Khidamat/al-Qaeda organization, from "Saudi Intelligence, the Saudi Red Crescent, the Muslim World League and Saudi princes and mosques.

In 1988, Naseef founded and chaired the MWL-spin-off, the Rabita Trust, which he chaired through 2001. It was a central charity in Pakistan (Saudi Arabia's most important ally other than Great Britain) and had a key role in the logistics for al-Qaeda and the Taliban. On October 12, 2001, the United States designated the Rabita Trust as a "Global Terrorist Entity" and froze its assets. On April 16, 2013, the Second Circuit U.S. Court of Appeals ruled that the suit brought by the families of the victims of 9/11 could proceed with discovery against Naseef, who the lawsuit states "knowingly provided financial support to al-Qaeda, through the MWL, Rabita . . . ." and other organizations.

Naseef is chairman of Prince Charles's Oxford Centre for Islamic Studies, and his close confidant.

• **Yusuf al-Qaradawi.** Al-Qaradawi served as a Trustee of the OCIS, at least through 2006.

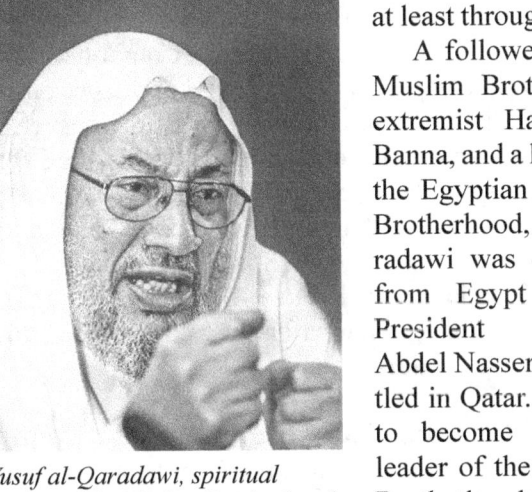

Yusuf al-Qaradawi, spiritual leader of the Muslim Brotherhood, and. . . bank advisor?

A follower of the Muslim Brotherhood extremist Hasan al-Banna, and a leader of the Egyptian Muslim Brotherhood, al-Qaradawi was expelled from Egypt by its President Gamal Abdel Nasser. He settled in Qatar. He rose to become spiritual leader of the Muslim Brotherhood worldwide, and according to his own account, was twice offered the post of official head of the Egyptian Brotherhood, but declined so as not to limit the scope of operations he could undertake. On Feb. 21, 2011, al-Qaradawi issued a fatwa against Libyan leader Muammar Qaddafi, who was later murdered. In 2011, al-Qaradawi entered Egypt to help direct the rise to power of the Muslim Brotherhood's pro-terrorist Mohammed Morsi.

After Morsi was removed from power during 2013 by Egyptian General Abdel Fattah el-Sisi, on July 22, 2013, al-Qaradawi appeared on the Qatari-controlled al-Jazeera news channel, to deliver a death threat, in particular against General el-Sisi, without mentioning his name, "if he, who has disobeyed the ruler [Morsi] does not repent, then he must be killed. There is a legitimate ruler [Morsi], and people must obey and listen to him." On June 1, 2103, al-Qaradawi called on radicalized Sunnis to flock to Syria to overthrow Bashar al-Assad.

• **Prince Turki bin Faisal bin Abdulaziz al-Saud.** Prince Turki is a Trustee of the Oxford Centre, and chairs its Strategy Advisory Committee, which develops the Centre's long-term strategy. From 1977 until September 2001, Prince Turki was the director of the feared al-Mukhabarat al-A'Amah, Saudi Arabia's Intelligence Service. Books and reports have linked Turki as a recruiter and confidant of Osama bin Laden, and a significant force in 9/11. Prince Turki is a long-time close friend and collaborator of Prince Charles. (Turki was one of the few foreign royals invited to Charles's 2005 wedding to Camilla Parker Bowles).

• **Prince Bandar bin Sultan al-Saud.** Prince Bandar was the architect of the al-Yamamah British weapons-for Saudi-oil deal, and while Saudi Ambassador to the U.S., was so close to the Bush family that he was known as Bandar Bush. He also considers Prince Charles one of his closest friends in the world. In 1990, Prince Bandar contributed funds to the Centre. In 1997, Bandar organized Saudi King Fahd to

Kremlin Presidential Press and Information office
Prince Bandar bin Sultan, in Moscow July 31, 2013

make an astounding £20 million contribution—approximately $32.4 million—to the Centre. The May 30, 1997 the *Financial Times* reported that the contribution was made at a private dinner held by Prince Charles in Eng-

Prince Charles does a sword dance in Saudi Arabia, February 2014.

Centre, shows the high regard [for it] by royalty," i.e., the Houses of Windsor and Saud.

The East London Mosque is more than just a place of worship: The United Kingdom Department of Communities and Local Government, an official agency of the government, reported that "the East London Mosque [is] the key institution for the Bangladeshi wing of JI [Jamaat-e-Islami] in the UK." The Jamaat-e-Islami is the institution for murderous terrorism on the Indian sub-continent, ravaging principally India, Pakistan, and Bangladesh. The Mosque has also been, at times, a breeding ground for Wahhabism.

land, with Bandar selected as the person to announce the gift.

Prince Charles and Prince Mohammed al-Faisal: Partnership in Destabilization

Prince Charles's friendship and working relationship with Prince Mohammed al-Faisal, dates back at least 15 years, and may date earlier to the late 1980s. Mohammed is the senior member of the al-Faisal family clan, one of the most evil and powerful of the inner clique of Saudi royal families that run the House of Saud dictatorship. They are all children of former Saudi King Faisal al-Saud (reigned 1964-75).

Around 1999 or 2000, Prince Charles and Prince Mohammed agreed to be the joint heads of the committee that raised the money to construct the *London Muslim Centre*, which was a physical addition of the *East London Mosque*, which allowed the mosque to hold an additional 15,000 worshippers. The East London Mosque, London's oldest, features a Muslim Brotherhood network. These two princes' working relationship dates from this period, although it may go back more than a decade earlier.

The East London Mosque's trust, in a history of itself, wrote "On the 23rd of November 2001, His Royal Highness, the Prince of Wales and His Royal Highness Prince Mohamed al-Faisal laid the foundation-stone of the London Muslim Centre as part of a ceremony to launch the construction project" Later, the East London Mosque boasted that "the presence of these two high-profile figures, at the launch of the London Muslim

The Financial Angels of Jihad?

At a January 8, 2015 Capitol Hill press conference, on the subject of the declassification of the 28 pages, former Senator Bob Graham, the co-chairman of the original 9/11 Congressional Inquiry Committee, who helped draft its report, laid particular importance on unearthing "the financial and other forms of support, of the institutions which were going to carry out those extreme forms of Islam" that culminated in 9/11. Senator Graham emphasized that those networks exist today.

Below we profile some Saudi-linked institutions whose affiliations have led to allegations of ties to terrorism, including, in numerous cases, by various government investigators.

Prince Mohammed al-Faisal's Banking Empire

Prince Mohammed al-Faisal, one of the many sons of Saudi King Faisal (reigned 1964-75), is considered to be Saudi Arabia's most significant banker, with a financial empire which extends across the world. His banking empire, however, has some very strange characteristics, as the following profiles show.

Prince Mohammed al-Faisal has established three major banking hubs: the Faisal Islamic Bank network, the Dar al-Maal al-Islami Trust (aka The DMI Trust), and the Faisal Private Bank. His flagship institution, the DMI, is a financial conglomerate, with approximately 20 offices around the world, including in offshore centers such as the Bahamas, and Luxembourg, the United Kingdom, Switzerland (where it was founded in 1981), Qatar, the U.A.E. and Pakistan. By 2012, DMI's assets under management reached the level of $6.5 billion.

The DMI Trust: DMI's initial directors and officers were extremely controversial individuals.

Ibrahim Mustafa Kamel. Ibrahim Kamel served as DMI's first chairman (he has no known connection to Saleh Abdullah Kamel, the current chairman and founder of the Dallah al-Baraka Group). On April 24, 2002, the United Nations placed Ibrahim Mustafa Kamel on its Security Council's Sanctions Committee listing pursuant to paragraphs 1 and 2 of resolution 1290 as being associated with al-Qaeda, and Osama bin Laden. The UN Security Council Committee then stated about Ibrahim Mustafa Kamel, that he "has provided material support in the form of manpower and other resources to enable the Islamic Army of Aden to pursue a terrorist agenda in Yemen.... The Islamic Army of Aden has also claimed involvement in the bombing of the USS Cole [which killed 17 American sailors] in Aden, Yemen, in October 2000."

Khalid bin Mahfouz served as member of DMI's board of directors. Mahfouz was a scion of the notorious Mahfouz dirty money banking family. Khalid bin Mahfouz acquired a 20% stake in and became a director of the Bank of Credit and Commerce International (BCCI). BCCI was eventually forced to liquidate, in the face of multiple investigations, in 1991. Authors Jonathan Beatey and S.C. Gwynne, in their book, *The Outlaw Bank: A Wild Ride Into the Secret Heart of BCCI*, wrote that BCCI's "black network" totaled between 1,000 and 1,500 people, and reportedly was used in terrorist ventures in countries around the world, including, according to the authors, the movement of narcotics to finance the Afghan mujahideen 'resistance.' Authors Peter Truell and Larry Gurwin stated in a September 2004 *Washington Monthly* article, that "law enforcement officials today acknowledge [that BCCI] would become a model for international terrorist financing."

In the early 1990s, when prosecutors from different countries forced the collapse of the BCCI bank, a large part of BCCI's "unrecorded deposits" were from Faisal Islamic Bank of Egypt, a sister bank of DMI as part of Prince Mohammed al-Faisal's banking empire.

Haydar Mohamed bin Laden, half-brother of Osama bin Laden, also served on DMI's board of directors. Haydar Mohamed bin Laden had set up a half-million dollar bank account in Geneva, Switzerland, payable to his brother Osama.

Hassan al-Turabi of Sudan served as a supervisory director of DMI Group from 1982 until 1992, according to an August 9, 2007 *New York Times* article. While he was an official in the Sudanese government, al-Turabi in 1992 helped arrange for Osama bin Laden to move to and live in Sudan, and provided him protection, as bin Laden established jihadi terrorist-training camps in Sudan.

Yusuf al-Qaradawi, whom we met above, served as DMI Trust's "Sharia advisor."

The Faisal Islamic Bank of Egypt. The Faisal Islamic Bank of Egypt in Cairo was established in the period 1977-79, as one of the first "Islamic" banks in the world. Not long thereafter, Mohammed al-Faisal set up its sister bank, the Faisal Islamic Bank of Sudan (the two of them together are here considered one bank). Again, Prince Mohammed's colleagues in this operations were controversial, to say the least.

Sheikh Omar Abdul-Rahman—the "blind Sheikh"—was a co-founder of the Faisal Islamic Bank of Egypt. During the 1970s, Abdul-Rahman simultaneously led the Egyptian Islamic Jihad, and the al-Gama'a al-Islamiyya, known simply as the Islamic Group. Never a banker nor a businessman, Abdul-Rahman has one "profession"—terror. The Egyptian government charged Abdul-Rahman with issuing the fatwa that resulted in the 1981 assassination of President Anwar Sadat by the Egyptian Islamic Jihad. He was acquitted of that charge, expelled from Egypt, and then went to went to Afghanistan where he helped build the *Maktab al-Khadamat, which would become al-Qaeda.*

By 1990, the U.S. State Department had placed Abdul-Rahman on its terror-watch list, but he managed to enter the United States three times between 1990 and 1992. Abdul-Rahman helped orchestrate the Feb. 26, 1993 New York City World Trade Center bombing, which, although intended to collapse both towers, ended up killing six people, and injuring about 1000. While not convicted of that bombing, Abdul-Rahman was arrested and convicted for a plot to blow up the United Nations, the Lincoln Tunnel, and the George Washington Bridge, and is currently serving a life sentence at the Butner Federal Correctional Institution in North Carolina.

The Faisal Private Bank: Founded under the name Faisal Finance in 1982 in Geneva, Switzerland, the bank changed its name to Faisal Private Bank around 1990. Prince Mohammed's DMI deployed a subsidiary—the Ithmaar Bank of Bahrein—which eventually acquired 100% of the stock of Faisal Private Bank of Switzerland.

Mohammed Galeb Kalje Zouaydi, the accountant for Prince Mohammed al-Faisal's sprawling banking empire, as well as for his brother Prince Turki, was arrested by Spanish authorities in 2002 and charged with being the principal funder of al-Qaeda activities in Europe. The May 6, 2002 *Chicago Tribune* reported that "The Spanish said the financier—Mohammed Galeb Kalaje Zouaydi—had ties to the cell in Germany that carried out the Sept. 11 attacks. Zouaydi is believed to have funneled money to al-Qaeda operations around the world, and Spanish authorities detailed transfers totaling $600,000." The referenced German cell was supposed to be that of Mohamed Atta, one of the 9/11 hijackers.

Osama Bin Laden's Bank

The **Al-Shamal Islamic Bank**, founded in Khartoum, Sudan in 1983, is often called "Osama bin Laden's bank," and with justification, as the U.S. State Department reported that Osama invested $50 million into the bank. It has been alleged that Bin Laden was one of its founders.

Reporter John Crewdson, reports in the Nov. 3, 2001 *Chicago Tribune*, in an article entitled "Swiss Officials Freeze Bank Accounts Linked to Supporters of Terrorist Groups" that,

"The al-Shamal bank does acknowledge that among its five 'main founders' and principal shareholders is another Khartoum bank, the Faisal Islamic Bank of Sudan." This is the Faisal Islamic Bank founded and owned by Prince Mohammed bin Faisal (above).

Al-Shamal's role in facilitating Bin Laden's activities was elicited in testimony in a federal trial in the Southern District of New York in 2001, and included transfers to finance purchase of a plane, and payments to al-Qaeda operatives.

Another Saudi Genocide

May 16—According to contacts of *EIR* in Sana'a, Yemen, the genocide against the population by Saudi Arabia's war machine is horrific. Among the reports that are considered reliable is one from the U.S.-based Freedom House that was provided by internal—not international observers—because international personnel are prevented from working inside the country due to continued Saudi bombardment.

Even more devastating is the fact that the almost total destruction of the transport, water, fuel, and power infrastructure can rapidly result in mass-killing of the population. Urgent humanitarian assistance is required both to address immediate human needs, and to repair the destroyed infrastructure.

According to the summary of the "6th Statistical Report from Freedom House, Yemen," that covers up through May 12, the bombing has resulted in:

• 3,979 civilian casualties. 571 are children below 15 years of age, and 249 are women;

• 6,887 injured. Among them 1,106 children below 15 years of age, and about 775 women;

• Bombing of 674 populated areas and demolishing of 7,021 houses; 143 houses destroyed with their inhabitants inside;

• 160,000-170,000 families emigrated from the targeted cities and villages;

• destruction of 931 civilian buildings, utilities, and basic infrastructure;

• 54 hospitals and health institutions, 26 mosques, and 168 educational institutions have been targeted, including 3 schools that were destroyed when the students were inside.

Notes on the compiling of the report point out that the report is about civilian casualties and damage from Saudi-led airstrikes, and clashes between armed militants and Yemeni army and security forces. The armed militants mentioned in this report are: the al-Houthi group (Ansar Allah); Saudi-backed ex-President Hadi's armed groups; and al-Qaeda armed groups. Most of the deaths and casualties are caused by the Saudi air attacks.

In reality, there has been no Saudi ceasefire, despite the propaganda promises from Riyadh over the last week, and at Obama's meeting with the Gulf Cooperation Council at Camp David May 14, there was a total coverup of the genocide.

—*Michele Steinberg*

Al-Rajhi Bank and the Golden Chain

In July 2012, the Senate Permanent Subcommittee on Investigations released a 330-page report detailing the ties of the British bank HSBC (formerly the Hong Kong and Shanghai Banking Corporation) to international narcotics money laundering and terrorist financing. The report led to a Justice Department investigation, that ended with a deferred prosecution agreement and a record nearly $2 billion in fines.

Nearly 50 pages of the Senate report were devoted to HSBC's role in terrorist financing. The report used as an example its corresponding relations with Al-Rajhi Bank, the largest Saudi bank with $59 billion in assets, documenting what the reports authors said were systemic HSBC failures to acknowledge U.S. government and other reports of al-Rajhi's links to Islamic extremists and terrorists.

The bank's founder and largest shareholder, Sulaiman bin Abdul Aziz al-Rajhi (SAAR), was named in 2002 as a member of the Golden Chain, a network of 20 leading financiers of al-Qaeda. Individual members of al-Qaeda banked at Al-Rajhi Bank. In 2003, the CIA issued a classified report entitled, "Al Rajhi Bank: Conduit for Extremist Finance," and, in the wake of 9/11, U.S. federal agents raided the Northern Virginia offices of the al Rajhi-linked SAAR Foundation, as part of Operation Green Quest, a law enforcement operation directed at alleged funders of jihadist terrorism.

While the bank and the al-Rajhi family have condemned terrorism and repeatedly denied any involvement in terrorist financing, the links between HSBC and al-Rajhi cited by the U.S. Senate investigators are a strong reminder of the British-Saudi ties which have been a recurring pattern in the probe of terrorist financing.

In a semi-official biography, Prince Bandar bin Sultan, a central figure in the suppressed 28-page chapter from the Joint Congressional Inquiry into 9/11, boasted that it was the special ties between the British and Saudi monarchies that allowed for the creation of the al-Yamamah deal. It is just that deal which, *EIR research* has shown, created the offshore slush funds that have financed Anglo-Saudi covert operations since the mid-1980s, including the Afghan mujahideen, from which many of the future jihadist terrorist organizations, including al-Qaeda, and the more recent Islamic State (ISIS) sprang.